Mastering Marriage

For Every Couple Who Wants to Grow
Happier and More in Love Each Year

Mastering Marriage

For Every Couple Who Wants to Grow Happier and More in Love Each Year

Charlie Michaels & Mike Brown

Mastering LifeSkills Inc.
Westerville, OH

Portions of this book were previously included in *Avoiding Wedding Aftershock* ©1990 Charlie Michaels & Mike Brown ISBN: 0-9626525-0-4

The following are trademarks of Charlie Michaels & Mike Brown: "Marriage Masters," "The Marriage Masters Movement," "for every couple who wants to grow happier and more in love each year," "I pick you," "Happily married and proud of it," "The Marriage Pact," "Emotional Prenuptial," and "The Web site for happy couples by happy couples."

FIRST EDITION

Library of Congress Control Number: 2005930361

ISBN: 978-0-9626525-1-6

Names and identifying characteristics of people in the book have been changed to protect their privacy.

Mastering LifeSkills books are available at special quantity discounts for religious organizations, marriage professionals, Marriage Masters™ groups, educational programs, to use as premiums and sales promotions, and for training programs or fundraising. For more information, please write to:
Director of Special Sales, Mastering LifeSkills Inc,
PO Box 1766, Westerville, OH 43086-1766.
Phone: 614-334-6627

Jacket design by George Foster
Editing by Audrey Glick
Cartoons by Charlie Michaels
Authors' photo by Carl Skanderup

DISCLAIMER:
THE FINE PRINT

This book is intended for couples in a good relationship who want to make it even better. It is not intended for couples with serious problems. The authors are not licensed marriage counselors. Nothing suggested is intended to take the place of a therapist, lawyer, accountant or other professional. If you need the help of an expert, please seek out a competent professional.

Neither the authors nor the publisher should be construed to be rendering legal, financial, clinical, medical or other professional advice. The authors gained the wisdom shared in this book by ceaselessly implementing these strategies over their 24+ years of marriage. Despite facing many challenges during these years, they have grown happier and more in love with each passing year. Consider the information in this book as the input of a valued friend.

Neither the publisher nor the authors assume responsibility for errors or omissions, nor shall the authors or publisher have liability or responsibility to any person or entity with respect to any loss or damage caused, or alleged to be caused, directly or indirectly by the information contained in this book.

The quotes contained in this book were collected over a long period of time from many sources including the Internet. When a source appeared with the quote, we acknowledge the reported author. Some sources were never known to us and we apologize for not being able to credit the author.

It simply isn't true, as some insist, that
"that little piece of paper doesn't make any difference."
It makes a tremendous difference.
Just think of how differently
you would regard an appeal for help from
a) your daughter's boyfriend or
b) your son-in-law.
Marriage matters, and so does the fact that
we are forgetting how much it matters.

The Washington Post Writers Group

DEDICATION

To every couple who understands their
marriage matters and is willing
to assume responsibility for its success.

The following pages reflect the steps we've taken to grow happier and more in love throughout our 24⁺ year marriage. We share them in hopes that your results will exceed your dreams and expectations as much as ours have.

In every marriage more than a week old,
there are grounds for divorce.
The trick is to find, and continue to find,
the grounds for marriage.

Robert Anderson

CONTENTS

CONTENTS, cont.

CONTENTS, CONT.

*Example is not the main thing in influencing others.
It is the only thing.*

Albert Schweitzer

OUR MISSION:

TO STRENGTHEN FAMILIES BY HELPING COUPLES GROW HAPPIER AND MORE IN LOVE EACH YEAR

School does little to teach us how to prepare for, create and maintain happy, healthy and enduring marriages. We are determined to change this by sharing tips and techniques for creating and maintaining a strong, satisfying marriage.

This book is the first step of our two step approach. In these pages we provide the practical advice couples need to elevate a good marriage to a great marriage. This advice has been time-tested by couples who actually have created successful marriages. Think hands-on, immediately applicable life skills that have worked for others.

On-going maintenance of a happy marriage is the goal of the second step of our approach, The Marriage Masters Movement˝. This grass roots organization is for couples who are committed to taking responsibility for the long-term success of their marriages.

At the heart of this organization is an on-line resource, www.MarriageMasters.com. On this site, happily married couples will share their tips and techniques to create marriages that meet the needs of both partners. It will also provide a forum for members to exchange ideas on a variety of topics. Membership is free. We invite every couple who wants to grow happier and more in love throughout a life-long marriage to join us in this cyber community. Share what has worked for you; read what has worked for others.

Please act on your commitment to your marriage by implementing the simple techniques in this book. Then, enlist in this ongoing maintenance program.

The more you invest in a marriage,
the more valuable it becomes.

Amy Grant

YOU'RE THE BEST!

We really want those who have contributed both directly and indirectly to the evolution of this book to know how much we appreciate their input:

First and foremost to Ken Burley, who suggested to Charlie that writing down and comparing our assumptions about marriage would be "a useful exercise." This was the best wedding present anyone could have given us. Ken and his wife, Mary, demonstrated that this concept, combined with integrity, can keep you happily married for over 60 years.

The Rev. Dr. Louis Gishler, an interim minister at The Village Church of Northbrook, Illinois, who married us. When we first learned that the regular minister was unavailable to perform our ceremony, we were disappointed to have to settle for a "stand in." What a blessing this turned out to be! During the service he surprised us by including a Scottish tradition; he wrapped our joined hands in a cloth and reminded us that we would need to choose to be married

What is a friend? I'll tell you.
It is a person with whom you dare to be yourself.

Anonymous

to each other each and every day in order for our marriage to succeed. This advice led to our discovering The 3 Most Important Words in Marriage (Clue #1).

Phil and Penny Wanzek and Bill and Betty Brown for being great parents.

Shirley, my Dad's second wife, for making my Dad happy.

Our grandparents, aunts and uncles, who demonstrated that most of the time a loving marriage isn't a 50/50 proposition.

Special thanks to Kathy Westman Figler, who introduced us.

Our children and their families for their love and support (as they appeared in our world): Andi, Christina, Anthony, Brian, Wendell, Isabella, CC, Treg, Libby and Claire.

Mike's first wife, Sally, and her husband, Jerry, for their friendship and for doing such a great job with the kids.

Those friends and acquaintances who marveled at the power of our marriage and encouraged us to write this book.

Our support team, which has provided emotional and technical support and appropriate distractions from this task (in alphabetical order because we want to remain on good terms with all of them): Tom Antion, Jack Barnard, Judith Beay, Jamie Bright, Anthony Brown & the team at Hoy Surveying, Christine Zahner Cohen, Andi & Wendell Dalton, Dick & Pam Eastman, Diane Edwards, George Foster, Randy Gilbert, Elizabeth & Wayne Gilham, Audrey Glick, Harvey Glick, Bill Harrison, Steve Harrison, John Kremer, Erin Leavitt, Channing and Julee Licon, Darla Lord, Peggy McColl, Christina & Brian Miller, Jen & Lou Nagy, Avra Mouzakis, Ellen Reid, Joel Roberts, Carl Skanderup, Peter & Cathy van der Horst, Steve Wanzek, Sarah Weinstock, Elaine Wilkes, Susan Willingham, Nancy Woods and Barbara Zahn.

Thank you all.

*The perfect marriage begins
when each partner believes
they got better than they deserved.*

Source Unknown

PART I

BY WAY OF
INTRODUCTION

Marriage is like twirling a baton, turning handsprings or eating with chopsticks. It looks easy till you try it.

Helen Rowland

CHAPTER 1

WHY READ *THIS* BOOK?

You are going to be so happy you picked up this book!

Okay, so picking up the book won't make you happy. But reading this book and implementing any combination of the clues we share with you will make you happier. The more of them you implement, the happier you'll be. And those of you who implement all of the ideas in this book are going to be happier than you can imagine.

How can we be so sure? Because we know these strategies work. We've lived them for a quarter of a century.

Some of these time-tested gems were passed along to us by couples who'd been married as long as 60 years. Most, we devised ourselves during our marriage. Others are just plain common sense, once you look at things from the right perspective.

If experience is the best teacher, you are learning from experts! You'll have a chance to read our story later, but suffice it to say, we've been around the block and have the battle scars to prove it.

Despite the exceptionally poor relationship skills we started off with and all the ups and downs we've faced together, our relationship has grown stronger every year. We both consider ourselves happier than we were when we first married – and we were on Cloud Nine then!

By the way, my name is Carol, but I prefer to go by my nickname, Charlie. My husband's name is Mike. When Mike and I married, we wanted our relationship to be different from those in our pasts. We wanted our "forever" to last our lifetimes, and we wanted to continue to experience the same level of joy we had found with each other while we were dating.

Neither of us had an extreme makeover in appearance, attitude, beliefs or behaviors. Yet, virtually overnight, our relationship skills improved and we were able to set aside the self-defeating behaviors that had plagued us in the past. You can do this, too. And, if you haven't suffered from self-defeating behaviors, you can avoid developing them.

Why have we been successful? Because we did everything we're sharing with you in this book. We consciously chose to tweak a few of our actions, focus our mind-set and align our expectations. And, perhaps most importantly, we have had the integrity to keep our word.

In these pages you will discover the blueprint for what we do that has been so successful for us, and we'll show you how to implement these actions in your marriage.

Whether you are married, engaged or just thinking about getting married, the ideas in this book will help you identify exactly what it is that each of you wants out of marriage and help you get it.

As you implement these ideas, you will grow and mature individually, as well as together, as a couple. You will gain better direction, have a better sense of appreciation for your partner and pick up immediately applicable skills that will have far-ranging impact on your marriage. And, if you're getting re-married, this book is even more vital. After all, you know things don't always work out the way you hoped they would.

We are so excited to share these ideas with you! They have the power to enrich your life and improve your happiness; they can make a good marriage great and a great marriage fabulous.

If you knew what to do to be happy, you'd do it, wouldn't you? Happiness is within your reach. We'll show you the way and give you the tools. But, ultimately, it's up to you to build the marriage that works for the two of you.

With best wishes for your success -

Charlie Michaels
AKA Mrs. Michael Brown

Mike Brown

Notes:

To eliminate the confusion of saying he/she, him/her, etc., We've alternated using he/him for one example and she/her for the next. No special meaning is intended.

Please think of references to you as yourself, any reference to he, she, him, her, guy, girl or spouse as your partner.

This book is for couples considering marriage, as well as those who are already married. Please adapt references to marriage, partnership or relationship to your relationship with your partner.

BY WAY OF INTRODUCTION

---

*You're given all these lessons for the unimportant
things: piano playing, typing, kickball.
You're given years of instruction on how to
balance equations -- something most people
never use in normal life.
But what about marriage?
Before you can drive a car you need
an approved course of instruction.
But driving a car is nothing, nothing
compared to living day in and day out
with your spouse!*

Source Unknown

CHAPTER 2

ALL YOU REALLY NEED TO KNOW ABOUT MARRIAGE YOU CAN LEARN FROM YOUR CAR

Maintaining a marriage is just like maintaining a car. You don't have to understand how to tear apart an engine or rebuild a transmission to keep your car in great shape. Your job, as the car owner, is to give the car regular maintenance, keep it fueled, maneuver it properly to avoid dings and dents, follow the rules of the road so your license isn't taken away from you and drive responsibly to avoid accidents. At regular intervals, you give it a tune-up.

With marriage, you don't need to understand relationship theory to keep your marriage in great shape. Your job, as a spouse, is to give your marriage regular attention, keep it fueled with love and passion, be gentle with each other to prevent physical and emotional damage, follow the rules you have laid down for your marriage so your marriage license isn't revoked, and behave kindly and responsibly to avoid major problems. At regularly scheduled intervals, give your relationship a tune-up.

This book is designed to help you keep your marriage running smoothly. It contains tips and techniques to take good care of your marriage and maintain it properly, establish the rules for your marriage and give your marriage a tune-up. You will discover, as we did, that a properly maintained marriage is a happy marriage.

"Mastering Marriage" is the term we've coined for developing the skills needed to create and maintain a successful marriage. You get to define what a successful marriage means to the two of you. We call couples who are dedicated to mastering marriage "Marriage Masters™."

In these pages, we've included everything we did to lay the groundwork for our relationship, as well as the things we do on a daily basis, that help us keep our love fresh and exciting. There are, undoubtedly, other ways to tend a marriage, but we don't know them! These techniques have worked for us and others, and we believe they will work equally well for you.

We started asking young couples at our clinic, "Who's marriage would you like yours to be like?" They'd answer, "We don't know any."

Jennifer Baker, when asked why she had become involved in Smart Marriages

---

A great relationship is not just for the two of you. Whether you are aware of it or not, your marriage is a role model for everyone who sees it. So a great relationship is also for your children, nieces, nephews, grandchildren, your children's friends, siblings and coworkers.

ALL YOU REALLY NEED TO KNOW ABOUT
MARRIAGE YOU CAN LEARN FROM YOUR CAR

Want your children to get a head start on success in life? Give them an example of a happy, loving marriage. This is the best gift you can give them. Not only does this provide a secure environment for emotional development, but your children will observe the skills they will need to create happy, healthy, mutually-fulfilling relationships when they grow up.

Please choose to accept responsibility for the success of your marriage. Give the next generation an example they will want to emulate; you never know who will be impacted by what you do.

Don't worry that children never listen to you;
worry that they are always watching you.

Robert Fulghum

About ten years ago, we lived in the front unit of a duplex. The young man who lived behind us had to walk past our kitchen window to get to his home. When we were making dinner or doing dishes, we frequently saw him with his girlfriend as they passed our window.

One day, the young lady tapped on our door. She wanted us to know that "the great example we'd set" had given them the courage to get married. I congratulated her and tried to minimize our role in their engagement. She was adamant; they didn't know many people who were happily married. Seeing the way we interacted and the love we had for each other after years of marriage gave them hope to believe it could be that way for them as well.

Poor examples can also have far reaching effects. If you know couples who are less than blissfully married, you probably recognize issues you will absolutely not tolerate in your own marriage.

We have a friend who is one of five children. From his perspective, his parents had a loveless marriage. He believes this poor example resulted in 13 marriages spread among his four siblings and him. None of them wanted a marriage like Mom and Dad's. When they recognized one of their parents' traits in their marriage, they bailed out.

---

*If love isn't taught at home,
it's difficult to learn it anywhere.*

Author Unknown

Just like every other skill, mastering marriage requires ongoing practice. This isn't drudgery, mind you, but an on-going intention to fine tune one's skills and improve one's finesse. Think Tiger Woods practicing a particular golf shot hundreds of time in a day. Think Yo Yo Ma repeating a musical passage over and over on his cello.

People who excel at their trade practice daily and enjoy it. Marriage takes this same commitment. It also takes courage, strength, willpower, resolve and a steadfast determination to create a happy life together.

If you are faint of heart, weak-willed or lazy, you might as well pack it in now, because you're not going to make it, at least not happily.

That said, we also believe that any two people who love each other and have the integrity to keep their word can create a highly satisfying marriage. Regardless of what your background is or how you came to where you are today, if you and your partner are prepared to accept responsibility for the success of your marriage, you can succeed.

Please be assured that the rewards of a happy marriage are well worth the time, energy and effort invested. This is an exciting process. It's a life-long adventure. The two of you are the center of your universe. Take proper care of your marriage and make your universe a happy place in which to live.

---

*There is no greater happiness for a man
than approaching a door at the end of a day
knowing someone on the other side of that door
is waiting for the sound of his footsteps.*

Ronald Reagan

---

*Most people get married believing a myth - that marriage
is a beautiful box full of all the things
they have longed for: companionship,
sexual fulfillment, intimacy, friendship.
The truth is that marriage, at the start, is an empty box.
You must put something in
before you can take anything out.
There is no love in marriage;
love is in people and people put it into marriage.
There is no romance in marriage;
people have to infuse it into their marriages.
A couple must learn the art and form the habit of giving,
loving, serving, praising- keeping the box full.
If you take out more than you put in, the box will empty.*

J. Allen Petersen, *Points to Ponder*

CHAPTER 3

THE MIRAGE OF "MARRIAGE"

When I think of a mirage, I envision a dying man crawling across the desert in search of water. Suddenly he sees a beautiful pool of cool water encircled by palm trees. As he approaches, the pool vanishes only to reappear at another point on the horizon.

Most of us approach "Marriage" while suffering comparable illusions. While my mirage of marriage undoubtedly differs from yours, we all have them. We denote the mirage of marriage as "Marriage," which should be read "marriage with a capital 'm'."

Many people believe that being "Married," in and of itself, is a state worth achieving. I'm assuming that all those people who hounded me with inane questions like, "Why isn't a nice girl like you married?" suffered from this illusion.

Some people believe "Marriage" will complete them and make them whole. Others believe that their partner will suddenly be morphed into a better human being or that "Marriage" will bring them the financial security, emotional stability, respectability and fulfillment they crave.

"Marriage" is believed by many to endow individuals with status, power, physical assets, happiness, wisdom and maturity, which is why so many people want to be "Married."

Why? Who wouldn't want to be like (depending on your era) Ozzie and Harriet Nelson, Mike and Carol Brady, Cliff and Clair Huxtable, Phillip and Vivian Banks or Eric and Annie Camden?

Here's another reason you may not have considered, a craving to be part of something - or at least not to be invisible. When you finish school, you face a huge void. Suddenly the creation of your world is totally up to you. While you may have been anxious to put school behind you and become independent, the reality of life without feedback is extremely difficult. Report cards may have been a great cause of angst, but at least someone knew you existed.

To fill this void, many people get married. We unconsciously expect "Marriage" to provide all the signposts, celebrations, pats on the head, badges, diplomas, blue ribbons, report cards, fun escapes, human contact, experiences and emotions our earlier life provided.

Why is it that people get married? Because we need a witness to our lives. There's a billion people on the planet. What does any one life really mean? But in marriage, you're promising to care about everything. The good things, the bad things, the terrible things, the mundane things. All of it...all the time, every day. You're saying "You life will not go unnoticed because I will notice it. Your life will not go unwitnessed - because I will be your witness."

Wife in the movie, "Shall We Dance?" 2004
Screenplay by Audrey Wells

Unfortunately, more than half of all marriages fail and of those couples who stay together, another 50% say they are not happy. What goes wrong?

It was surprising to us that we couldn't find definitive statistics on why marriages fail. Following is an alphabetical compilation of reasons we found after searching the Internet.

- Abuse: physical, sexual, emotional, drugs or alcohol
- Failed expectations
- Financial problems
- Lack of commitment to marriage (Yikes! One study identified this as the greatest contributing factor in 85% of all divorces.)
- Infidelity
- Poor communication skills
- Poor conflict resolution skills
- Sexual incompatibility
- Unmet needs

Does this list contain the issues you expected?

I'd go along that this is what people believe causes their divorce, but I truly feel most of these reasons are just excuses. I believe most marriages fail because the partners were expecting too much from "Marriage."

If you want to remain happy and in love, it's critical that you understand that marriage provides nothing that you and your spouse don't put into place yourselves.

If you don't put something into your marriage above and beyond your physical presence, you will get little satisfaction and find little happiness there. Expecting "Marriage" to fill the voids in your life or do anything for you without your input is the first step toward disillusionment.

Marriage does NOT automatically provide financial security,

The big lie: Nothing will change when we marry.

emotional stability, mental health, kindness, love, friendship, an escape from loneliness, sex, happiness, good times, children, extended family, happy holidays, soul mate or even someone to live with. Marriage doesn't give you the opposite of these things either.

The point is marriage, in and of itself, gives you the opportunity for everything but the assurance of nothing. Your marriage can be whatever you want it to be. But it takes conscious thought and a bit of planning to develop these attributes.

Would you like your marriage to last the rest of your life? Would you like both you and your spouse to be glad you're married to each other all those years? Are you willing to do a bit of work today and everyday to greatly improve the chances of making your marriage not only survive, but thrive?

We certainly hope so. The balance of this book is designed to help you create a marriage that is just what the two of you want it to be. In the process, you'll also avoid the stumbling blocks that many people blame for the failure of their marriages.

Part II of this book will help you sharpen your relationship skills. In the event that you are lacking in relationship skills as both Mike and I were, pay close attention and really work hard on this section. We know from experience that conscientiously implementing the tips and techniques shared in our Clues will give you the skills you need to make virtually any relationship work, not just your marriage.

You MUST implement these suggestions for them to have any impact on your life. I promise you that with sufficient practice they will become second nature to you.

In Part III, you will learn to replace "Marriage" with a realistic view of marriage that you and your partner will look forward to sharing together. It makes no difference to your ultimate success where you are now in your relationship. If you and your partner want to create a great life together, you can do it.

Your biggest obstacle may be giving yourself permission to change. This was a huge barrier for me. For me, to be kind and loving to Mike told the world how much I cared about him. I felt so vulnerable. Sounds pathetic, doesn't it? But it still chokes me up to think about this difficult adjustment. In retrospect, it felt wonderful to allow someone to get emotionally close to me. But at the time, it was the scariest thing I'd ever done.

Human beings, who are almost unique in having the ability to learn from the experience of others, are also remarkable for their apparent disinclination to do so.

Douglas Adams

CHAPTER 4

WHO ARE WE
TO TELL YOU ANYTHING?

Mike and I are ordinary people with an extraordinary gift to share with you: the clues to growing happier and more in love throughout your marriage. We hope you share them with others.

We didn't start out as likely candidates to be writing a book on this topic. My dating history goes from comical to sad to really pathetic. At my high school graduation dinner, my classmates named me "The person most likely to have her love life made into a soap opera." And they knew me before things got bad!

Ultimately, I was angry, hurt and both hated men and needed their approval. I had no positive relationship role models and no apparent relationship skills. I am a perfectionist as well as bossy, demanding, strong willed, impatient and intolerant of nonsense. I have some positive traits, I'm sure.

Mike doesn't really have a dating history. He went to an all boys' high school and admits to being completely backwards and awkward with women. He has an explosive temper and is a perfectionist. He is also bossy, argumentative, demanding, strong willed, work obsessed, impatient and intolerant of nonsense. His need to excel at work caused him to put in 15 to 18 hour days at the office and destroyed his first marriage. His grandparents' marriage was a great role model, but his parents' marriage was stormy and competitive.

Like most couples getting ready to marry, we were happy and in love but didn't have a clue how to stay that way. We had both lost at love before and we were determined not to repeat our mistakes. We didn't know where to begin, but we knew we wanted to enjoy each other in our marriage 'forever.' And, we wanted our 'forever' to last our lifetimes.

We spent a lot of time and effort developing strategies to keep our marriage thriving and fulfilling. Twenty-five years later these strategies are still working for us. This was a deliberate plan of action we implemented. We're not talking about some esoteric theory we devised to reinvent ourselves, but simple steps we undertook that radically improved our relationship skills. We believe these simple strategies will work equally well for you.

---

*The greatest discovery of my generation
is that a human being can alter his life
by altering his attitude of mind.*

William James

WHO ARE WE TO TELL YOU ANYTHING?

Mike and I have worked hard to create a fabulous relationship. People have sometimes assumed that we must have lived on easy street to remain this devoted to each other after a quarter century. Quite the opposite.

- A few months after we married, we left well established business careers in Fortune 500 companies to start our own company. It failed.
- We sold everything we owned to pay business debts and child support and were $800 short of bankruptcy.
- Following our business failure, we took a series of odd jobs. We cleaned hotel rooms and did small home improvement projects. Mike drove a fork-lift at a warehouse while I worked at a fast food restaurant. At times we lived with relatives exchanging our labor for room and board.
- We moved to the town where Mike's children were so his son would live with us. Homework was a battle every night, but his grades came up. After a six month trial, he chose to return to his mother's home which just about broke Mike's heart.
- We traveled the country living on bologna sandwiches and camping out of our car for over a year while we decided where we would live.
- When Mike's mother became ill, we drove 4,200 miles in six days to get to Ohio from Alaska. We moved in and cared for her for six months to allow her to stay at home with her beloved dogs until she needed full nursing care. Did I mention that she didn't like me?
- Mike moved to a city he didn't like and took a job he didn't want so that I could pursue an acting career. Unless you attended the Los Angeles County Sheriff's training academy, you've never seen my work.
- My mother lived with us for five months of hospice care until

her death from brain cancer.

As I review the previous litany, I realize I haven't touched on my eight year bout with untreated clinical depression, Mike's broken bones and chronic back pain, my thyroid problems, our infertility and unsuccessful attempts to have a baby, our twelve year remodeling project, or the winter we lived in an unheated house without a back wall or roof because our demolition got ahead of the permitting of our plans for the renovation.

It's embarrassing to think how much more I could add to the above list. And, yes, in spite of it all, it has been a great life. We feel incredibly blessed.

Love is what you've been through with somebody.

James Thurber

Any one of the above events could have destroyed a relationship. Why did ours not only survive, but thrive? We educated ourselves. We learned how to maintain our perspective, align our priorities and stay in touch with each other on mental, emotional and physical levels. Our education began when we acted on advice we received from a near stranger, Ken Burley. Ken was a consultant hired by my boss to work on a project I was directing.

Shortly after I met Ken, he took me aside and said he could tell just by looking at me that I had met the man I was going to marry. I was not impressed. In fact, I felt terribly transparent and threatened.

I hardly knew this man and here he was delving into my personal life. Despite my attempts to change the subject, he persisted. He insisted on sharing some advice that had allowed his wife and him to live happily together for over 48 years.

The love we have in our youth is superficial compared to the love that an old man has for his old wife.

Will Durant

As he compared himself with his wife Mary, I was shocked. She was devoutly Christian and he was an atheist. They were both exceedingly strong-willed and had so many other differences it was hard to imagine their interest in each other. Yet, they had created a life together that satisfied, rewarded and fulfilled both of them. He now had my full attention.

His advice was simple and direct. Prior to their engagement, they had individually and separately written out their expectations for their relationship. They compared their personal expectations and agreed on how they would handle their differences. For nearly fifty years, their integrity in upholding these agreements had enabled these two tremendously different individuals to delight in a highly satisfying marriage. They revisited their agreements many times; some they changed, but many remained constant.

Now I was really irritated! At first I didn't even want to talk about this topic, and now I was not only intrigued, I was envious. I wanted what Ken and Mary had. I wanted to be me but I wanted to be me in a relationship of that quality.

Ken believed any two people could create a satisfying relationship by following this advice. I wasn't so sure. I'd never experienced a happy, healthy relationship. It seemed doubtful that the simple plan he outlined could dramatically change my luck with men.

Intuitively, I bought into the theory behind Ken's advice. It made a lot of sense that if you worked out your differences in advance, you wouldn't have them crop up later and cause problems. I loved this idea! I'm a conflict avoider big-time. The thought that conflict could pretty well be eliminated from a relationship by spending a bit of time upfront had obvious advantages. But doubts about the potential effectiveness of the idea remained, and I never expected to have a chance to give his suggestion a try.

When things ultimately did get serious between Mike and me (whom I'd met shortly before Ken told me I'd met the man I was going to marry), I shared Ken's advice with him and suggested we give it a try.

I wanted to give our marriage every chance of getting off on the right foot, but I didn't really think Mike would be interested in putting our relationship under such scrutiny. I was wrong; he was. In fact, he thought it sounded like a very good idea.

We decided the idea merited a long weekend. In preparation, we individually wrote out our assumptions on every topic that came to mind. I had 38 pages and Mike had eight!

Suddenly, I wasn't so sure I should have brought it up. Something inside me told me that when he finally knew all about me, he'd dump me! Talk about insecure! I still have the greeting card I bought to send him if we broke up.

*When I look back on all these worries I remember
the story of the old man who said on his deathbed
that he had a lot of trouble in his life,
most of which never happened.*

Sir Winston Churchill

Friday we began comparing our ideas.

It was an incredible three days: fun, heartwarming, endearing, hilarious, occasionally infuriating and a few moments of sheer panic. The things we learned about each other! No, we didn't agree on everything. But in our disagreement, it was thrilling to experience each other's commitment to our relationship.

We laughed, we cried, we shared hopes, dreams, secrets and fears that we had never trusted to anyone. Under all the passion and love we shared, we discovered that we really, *really*, REALLY liked each other.

Ultimately, we devised a list of mutual agreements, the result of negotiation and compromise. We called this our Marriage Pact™ and pledged to honor it.

It was the best investment either of us had ever made in a relationship. We eliminated many nagging doubts, honestly addressed problems we would face, nipped disagreements in the bud and set the stage to become best friends.

Ken's technique worked! And so did the other strategies we put into place. For nearly a quarter of a century we have lived happily without resentments, arguments or even serious disagreements. We have faced and overcome numerous challenges without ever feeling any threat to our relationship. In fact, our partnership has grown stronger with each adversity we've faced.

Over the years, we repeatedly thanked Ken and Mary for sharing this technique with us and told them they owed it to the world to share their message. Ken's reply was that someone else was going to have to do it, why didn't we? Indeed.

In 1990 we wrote a book, *Avoiding Wedding Aftershock or I Like You Even Better Now That I Know You*, to do just that. Unfortunately, our self-published volume never really got off the ground. We sold about two thousand copies before we ran out of money to promote it. A very limited, but loyal following of clergy and marriage and family counselors, continue to purchase this book, but for the most part, the book is out of circulation.

When Ken and Mary died, we realized that some day we would be gone too and what would happen to this advice? The information is incredibly valuable. It was unthinkable that we would allow it to die with us. We decided to make a more concerted effort to make this information available to other couples.

So there you have it. Couples who read drafts of this book consistently said they benefited from the information regardless of the stage of their relationship: seriously dating, engaged, newlywed, happily-on-going, at a crossroads, even those together upwards of fifty years. We know there is something here for every couple. We challenge you to take action.

This is a practical, easy to implement, hands-on guide: no theories, hypotheses, anthropological studies or educational treatises. Just a simple system that worked for us.

We truly believe that any couple can duplicate our success.

WHO ARE WE TO TELL YOU ANYTHING?

These strategies are not complex. They are easy to understand and straightforward to implement, but you will need to practice them for the rest of your lives to have them work for you.

So, read on! Some of our ideas are so intuitive that you may begin practicing them without even thinking about their implementation. Others will take conscious thought, and a few will take a concerted effort to put into action. Each one of them will be well worth the time and effort invested.

Opportunity is missed by most people because it...looks like work.

Thomas A. Edison

---

*When couples marry they are happy and in love,
but most don't have a clue how to stay that way.*

*Here are the clues. If you follow them,
you will discover the means to grow happier and more in
love through the adventure of your marriage.*

Charlie & Mike

PART II

THE CLUES
TO MASTERING MARRIAGE

*To the world you may be one person,
but to one person you may be the world.*

Bill Wilson

THE 3 MOST IMPORTANT WORDS IN MARRIAGE

Next time you're in a crowded room, visually single out any other couple. It's shocking, but statistically speaking, if their marriage survives, yours won't. With more than 50% of all marriages failing, virtually everyone has seen the devastating effects divorce can have.

We came up with a way to help you dramatically beat these odds in just one second a day. Sounds too good to be true, doesn't it? But it really works. We call it our "Recommitment Race." I sometimes think we should call it our "One Second Life Preserver for Marriage," because it has really been a life saver for us. Here's how our Recommitment Race came about.

During our wedding ceremony, the minister expanded on the lessons he shared during our rehearsal. He reminded us how easy it is to get married when you're surrounded by the encouragement of family and friends, and how difficult it is to stay married once all the hoopla has quieted down. For our marriage to succeed, he said we would have to choose to be married to each other every day for the rest of our lives.

En route to the reception, we reminisced about the ceremony. The minister's talk made sense to both of us. We had no idea how we would do it, but we agreed to recommit ourselves to each other daily. That night we stumbled across an unexpected solution.

Following our wedding reception, Mike was hanging over the bathroom sink throwing up the effects of too many tequila shots with beer chasers. I was fuming. Cleaning vomit out of a sink was far from my image of marital bliss, and was WAY down the list of things I'd hoped to do on our honeymoon.

Sensing my ill humor, Mike looked up at me and blurted, "Do you still pick me?" Well, of course I said that I still picked him. The room was absolutely quiet for a moment and then we started laughing like idiots. All of a sudden it seemed to occur to both of us at the same time. We would use the phrase "I pick you" to recommit to each other every day.

Since that first day, we have picked each other every morning. At the sound of the alarm we race to see who can be first to say, "I pick you." Silly as it seems, these words never fail to get the day off to a great start with a smile on both our faces.

These words are even more effective when we've spoken harshly, been nasty or feel we may have disappointed the other person in some way. Then we'll ask, "Do you still pick me?"

It's amazing how the words "Yes, I still pick you" help us keep the insignificance of our disagreements in perspective. They remind us how much more important our relationship is than whatever the stupid thing was we were disagreeing about.

"I pick you" are the three most important words in our marriage. If you take only one idea from this book to incorporate into your rela-

Confirming your commitment to each other
helps keep things in perspective.

tionship, this is the one. It is the simplest and most effective advice you will ever receive.

It's difficult to describe how such simple words can become so important, but these words are incredibly powerful. Together we have decided they mean, "You are the most important person in my life. I love being married to you. If I had it to do all over again, I would. I still choose to be married to you."

Say "I pick you" (or your own version) to each other every day. It may feel awkward at first, but say it anyway. Give those words power. Choose to have them mean: I want to be here, I want you to be with me and I will abide by the agreements we have made.

Infatuation and intimacy ignite love,
commitment makes the flame keep on burning.

Source Unknown

Choose each other every day. Say "I pick you" and mean it. This daily affirmation of choosing each other pays off.
- It's not as easy to take each other for granted.
- Knowing your spouse still chooses you over all others makes you feel good about yourself.
- It's easier to communicate with someone you know loves you in spite of your shortcomings.
- It's tough to deceive or cheat on someone when you pledge your love, trust and loyalty to her daily (We think this is so neat!).
- It's easier to keep your promises because you rethink your

commitment daily.

- Removing self doubts encourages intimacy.
- It helps you maintain your perspective when you disagree.
- You'll feel loved right down to the tips of your toes.

We have consciously picked each other to be our partner every day for nearly a quarter of a century. Over the years, the process has become something of a game, while the underlying sentiments have intensified with greater meaning.

If one of us sees it's after midnight, he'll say, "I pick you" to the other who then says, "I pick you, too." Our rule is that you can only pick each other for one calendar day at a time, so the earlier in the day you pick each other, the longer you get each other that day. We always race to see who picks first, sometimes teasing that the one who picked first must have wanted the other more. When one of us travels, we pick each other daily by phone or, if time zones don't permit, in absentia.

Please add this to your daily routine: Say, "I pick you," turn off the alarm and get out of bed. It's so easy!

Don't think that saying, "I love you" is the same thing. It truly isn't. We tell so many people we love them that the meaning becomes diluted. Plus we love our cars, pets, hobbies, ad infinitum. Select a phrase you won't say to anyone else. One of our daughters and her husband say, "Choose you." The other daughter and her spouse, playing on their wedding vows, say, "I do choose you."

Of course we still say "I love you," but we've found that saying "I pick you" means "I love you" and so much more.

It is virtually impossible to convey the power these three simple words have in our marriage, but I can tell you this: we don't believe that any couple who recommits to each other each and every day will ever become a divorce statistic.

On a scale of 1 - 10, make your relationship a 10!

CLUE # 2

FIND TIME
TO BE MARRIED

Why is it that every couple manages to find time to date, and yet so few of us give our marriage similar priority? It's really quite simple; you found time to date, find time to be married.

People don't get married hoping to be number two or three in their spouse's life. I bet you didn't get married thinking

- "I look forward to my husband working late and playing golf on the weekends."
- "I want my wife to spend all her time on household chores, volunteering and taking the kids places."
- "I sure hope my wife starts traveling with her job. Then, if she'll just spend her free time at the mall, I'll never have to see her!"
- "I can't wait till we have our own home so my husband can spend every waking minute in his workshop."

Pretty crazy isn't it? Yet isn't that what seems to happen to many couples? Don't let this happen to you.

The first step in achieving success in marriage is agreeing to keep each other number one in your lives. This may sound obvious. You got married, didn't you? Of course your spouse is number one in your life. But, when the guys start kidding around and say, "You're whipped! Man, she's got you wrapped around her little finger." Or a friend says, "Watch out, girlfriend, he has got you under his spell. You are so being domesticated." It takes a self-assured, mature individual to acknowledge that, not only is that true, but that you hope those feelings last the rest of your life.

If you choose to give your marriage top priority, it will be natural to make choices that are in the best interest of both of you. It will also be natural to choose to spend free time with your spouse. If you devote three hours a week to playing sports or watching them on TV, doing needlework, working on a collection, tinkering in the garage or going out with your friends, plan to spend at least three pleasurable hours a week sharing common non-sexual interests with your partner. You need free time apart and you need time together.

The fact that you both are in the house or even in the same room doesn't mean you are spending time together. If one of you is reading the paper and the other is balancing the checkbook, you haven't spent time together even if you've been sitting side by side for four hours. Time you spend doing chores or working on projects that demand your complete attention does not count as time together.

What do you like to do together? Take walks? Work in the garden? Go to museums? Play cards? The key here is your mutual interests. If gardening is something you both enjoy, it counts; if it's a chore, it doesn't qualify.

You'll need to be honest with your partner about the satisfaction you derive from the different kinds of time you spend together. For some couples, enjoying a book in front of the fire or going out for dinner may be good quality time together. These don't work for us.

I can't hear over the ambient noise in restaurants, so I don't enjoy the social aspects of eating out. Mike doesn't consider reading as time spent together because I get so involved in my books that I hardly know he exists. It's what works for the two of you that matters.

When a demand for your time arises, you need to convince your spouse that this is a good use of your time. You must either agree that you will participate together or agree that you will take part alone. If you can't agree on your involvement, turn down the opportunity if you want to be happily married.

"We forgot to do the most important thing. We forgot to be married."

Lance Armstrong, seven-time winner of the Tour de France, writing about his failed marriage.

We are not advocating totally neglecting your family or friends. We are saying that your spouse's feelings should come before everyone else's, even if you feel your spouse is being a little unreasonable. Everything comes down to choices. Surprise!

When people ask you to bake for a fund-raiser, fix their car, visit Aunt Mildred in the hospital or go out for dinner, they are, in effect, asking you to give them priority over your spouse during that time. No one extends an invitation so you can spend quality time with your spouse; they invite you to spend quality time with them. You must decide what's best for you - the two of you.

There will be times when you want to be surrounded by other

people and there will be times when you need to be alone. It's unfortunate when your best friend's party comes on the first night the two of you have been home without commitments in two weeks. If it happens, we'd suggest that you call your friend and explain that you'll only be at the party for a short time. Make a brief appearance and then go home or out together. You need time alone together outside the bedroom.

To protect your relationships with friends and family, try our simple policy. If it's necessary to decline an invitation, always put the blame on the person with the closest relationship to the people who are being turned down. If it's your family, you take the blame. If you are turning down your spouse's friends, your spouse takes the blame. Your family and friends will forgive you more readily than your spouse.

It may seem easier to place the blame on your spouse: "I'd love to go, but you know how George feels about museums." Or, "Mary's not one to get her shoes dirty; we'll have to take a pass on a day at the lake." But this can cause them to harbor hard feelings toward your spouse. Eventually, relationships with your friends or family may become so strained that you find yourself avoiding them.

You can always honestly say, "I'm sorry we won't be able to join you. We have a prior commitment." This is always true, because you made a permanent commitment to each other when you married.

Children pose the greatest challenge to a couple's intention to keep each other number one. No matter how intense your love is for your child, you must choose to give your spouse emotional priority to keep your marriage healthy, happy and strong. One of the greatest gifts you can give your children is a great example of marriage and family life. If you want your children to grow up in a two parent family, make certain that you give your spouse emotional priority and make time to be with your spouse without your children. Spoil your spouse, not your children. Every family member benefits when Mom and Dad are happy. It may be helpful to keep in mind that your primary job as a parent is to prepare your children to live without you. After they leave, you and your spouse will still need each other... and someday you may be blessed with grandchildren to enjoy (they are the BEST!)

Putting your spouse ahead of your parents and other close family members can be difficult. You have a lifetime invested with Mom and Dad, your grandparents, aunts, uncles, siblings and cousins and they are used to having priority in your life. At first, this may take quite a bit of adjustment for everyone, but ultimately you are not responsible for their happiness and they are not responsible for yours. If they love you, they will want you to be happy in your marriage. This means they should encourage you to give your marriage and your spouse top priority.

It's incredibly easy to get caught up in an activity trap, in the busyness of life; to work harder and harder at climbing the ladder of success, only to discover it's leaning against the wrong wall.

Wood Sabold

Hobbies, pets and jobs can also compete for top billing. Don't allow them to precede your spouse. Mike gave his job more priority than he gave his first wife and it led to their divorce. He was putting in long hours at the office because he thought it would allow him to provide a better life for his family. Unfortunately, his devotion to work forced his wife to create a life that didn't include him. Eventually Mike and his wife became strangers sharing a house.

Don't do this to each other! Your spouse truly is your other half. Your parents have their own lives, your children will grow into lives of their own, your friends may move away. You may lose your job. Your pet will die. You will grow older and may no longer be able to pursue your hobby. The one person whose life is intimately intertwined with yours for all time is your spouse.

Although it may be a tough adjustment for you, your family, your friends and your boss, make your spouse number one in your life. When you give your spouse this emotional priority, you will find time to be married. Finding time to be married will get you well on your way to mastering marriage.

Decide what your priorities are and how much time you'll spend on them. If you don't, someone else will.

Harvey Mackay in *SAM's Club Source*

USE YOUR POWER LOVINGLY

Your spouse's love for you and his willingness to make you number one in his life gives you tremendous power over him. When you're number one, you can separate your partner from anything in the world: friends, family, habits, hobbies, possessions. You may know someone who has walked away from her family, her friends, her job, even her children for the sake of love. It's important to recognize the power you have been given and use it lovingly.

My dad blessed me with a wonderful example of a loving use of power which ultimately impacted my relationship with Mike's family. My grandmother didn't like my dad. He was of the wrong Christian denomination. He was motivated too much by money. I'm sure she had a whole litany of complaints from which I was kindly protected by my parents.

When we visited my grandparents, my grandmother would make snide comments and was generally mean to my dad. I could see this even as a child. I could also see the way my dad tempered his emotions. His face would be taut and his jaw clenched, but he said nothing in response to her jabs and did his best not to contribute to the tension. My mother's admonitions to my grandmother were ineffective, so pretty much everyone tried to ignore her comments.

My dad could have used his power to separate my mother from her family.

- He could have refused to join us in our visits to my grandparents which would have been humiliating for my mom. She would still have taken us to see them, but surely not as often.

- He could have made it very uncomfortable for my mother to visit her parents by making her choose between her love for him and her love for her parents.

- He could have refused to have his in-laws visit our home and my mother would not have invited them.

But, he did none of these things. Out of respect and love for my mother and his desire to allow his children to know their grandparents, he put up with my grandmother. I know my mother was aware of this sacrifice and I hope she told him how much she appreciated that he did this for the rest of us.

My dad's example of restraining his use of power strongly impacted our marriage. Mike's mother was similarly cruel to me. Following in my dad's footsteps, I put up with her verbal abuse so as not to get between Mike and his mother. An aside is worth mentioning here. Mike was not aware of his mother's comments. Because she was older and not well, I never told Mike about her cruelty. I knew he would not tolerate it and I didn't want to take away what little time they had left together. Had she been younger and healthier, I would have chosen to address this issue and put a stop to her comments.

If you are distressed by anything external, the pain is not due to the thing itself, but to your estimate of it; and this you have the power to revoke at any moment.

Marcus Aurelius

Here's another example, merging two households. I heard a friend bemoan the fact that her intended wanted to bring some hideous objects – an old chair, wagon-wheel coffee table and neon beer sign – with him into their marriage. In truth, she wasn't looking to merge household. She merely wanted to move her man and his clothes into her set-up.

To the best of my knowledge, this man parted with his cherished items. Was this an inappropriate use of power? How can someone expect to feel at home if his favorite things are taken away from him? If someone isn't feeling comfortable in his surroundings, it's a step toward disillusionment.

On a more playful note, many wives use their power to stop their spouses from looking at other women. I'm not sure why. You're married, but neither of you is dead. It's only natural to notice people who are out there working hard to be noticed. We have taken the "just because you're on a diet doesn't mean you can't enjoy the menu" approach to looking at attractive men and women. This works well for us. Neither one of us stares, points, makes wise cracks or does anything to embarrass our partner or the object of our admiration, but we do enjoy people watching together.

Mike might ask me to repeat something saying, "I'm sorry, a sweet young thing just walked through the door and I went temporarily deaf." I might say, "Look at that incredible hair on that blond in the red top," to which Mike might reply, "Sorry, I can't get past the red top." We'll both chuckle over this. I find it immensely flattering that Mike still picks me over these women who are absolutely gorgeous. Sometimes we'll pass someone with a body like Michelangelo's David and I'll be overwhelmed with admiration. We will share our opinions on his pecs and washboard stomach and vow to head to the gym.

Our openly admiring approach may not work for you. Still, think twice before you make a power play and forbid something. Be sure this is the best and most appropriate use of your power or you might win the battle and ultimately lose the war.

Sometimes your decisions affect people outside your marriage as in the following example which had long-range implications, not only for us and our marriage, but also for Mike's kids. Earlier, I shared the story of our business failure and near bankruptcy. As we worked multiple jobs to pay our bills, we had to decide how to spend the very small amounts of disposable income we were able to scrape together. Mike felt that I had sacrificed so much already for his child support and our other commitments that I should get to spend any excess money we had on something for me.

I am neither a saint nor a masochist. Of course I wanted to spend the money on me. But we hadn't seen Mike's children in nearly a year. It might easily be two, three, even five years until we could really afford to have them come visit us. By the time we could afford to have them visit, they might not want to come. I used my power literally to force Mike to squirrel away money for plane tickets for his children to visit us. He felt guilty doing it, but we both knew it was what needed to be done at the time.

You will find as you look back upon your life
that the moment when you have really lived
are the moments when you have done things
in the spirit of love.

Henry Drummond

It's easy to say that there is no right or wrong way to resolve an issue, but the truth is, some solutions are better than others. The best solutions are those that you both agree to follow amicably. Additionally, we feel it is wrong to force someone to do things your way or lord it over your spouse that you agreed to do things her way.

While you are not responsible for your spouse's happiness, if you use your power inappropriately, you may be directly responsible for your spouse's unhappiness. Use your power wisely and make decisions that will impact your lifetime together in a positive way.

You may find you become a prisoner
of your deceptions.

TRADING FACES

We all did things while we were dating to make ourselves more desirable, didn't we? We dressed up, we put on our best manners and we went places and did things that we'd never done before, and, in some cases, hoped we'd never have to do again.

When we were dating, Mike pretended to like broccoli, mushrooms and escargot. These foods could have been featured on his own personal "Fear Factor" episode. Once we got married, I learned that Mike is actually a meat and potatoes man. This was not only a big surprise, but also a disappointment, since it severely limited opportunities to experiment with my cooking and our dining out choices.

As Mike would be quick to point out, I dropped a few masks myself once we got married. My house was spotless when we dated. Mike was particularly impressed with my freezer which had a list on the door of every item inside and the date it was put there. Since we've been married, Mike has learned that I value expedience more than neatness. There have been times when my projects were so spread out on the floor it was impossible to tell if we had carpet.

Many of us carefully donned masks while we were dating to attract our partner. These masks hid the real us. We call dropping these masks after marriage "trading faces."

Why are so many of us guilty of trading faces? We were hoping to catch the eye and the interest of someone special. She noticed. You dated. You married. Did you ever stop to think that maybe some of those things you did that were out of character for you were the exact things that made your partner decide that you were the one?

- She's perfect. She loves to watch sports and action movies.
- He's perfect. He actually likes spending time with my family and doesn't mind shopping.

This can be a huge problem.

When you're dating, you are evaluating each other to see if you'd like to spend the rest of your lives together. If you aren't being yourself, with whom is she falling in love? Is it any surprise that people become disillusioned when the masks come off? Especially if, as sometimes happens, a spouse has changed so much after marriage that he seems to bear no resemblance whatsoever to the man she dated.

When you marry, each of you has a right to expect that what you saw of your partner prior to marriage will be what you will see in your married life. If you're not yet married, it's critical that you present yourself to your partner as the person you plan to be in your permanent relationship, essentially, the real you. If you exhibited out of character traits when you started dating, it's important to allow the real you, in all your glory, to emerge now, before you marry. This will prevent your spouse feeling he's been sold a bill of goods.

43 percent of married couples are not together within 15 years, and of those who do stay together, 4 in 10 say they're not happy. Warren estimates that three-quarters of marriages are in trouble the day they get started.

Neil Clark Warren
founder, eHarmony.com
quoted in *U.S. News and World Report*

If you're already married, it's only fair that you continue to do those out of character behaviors that appealed to your partner while you were dating, if they remain important to her. If you're not sure if your spouse is missing something you used to do, ask her. If you're missing things your spouse used to do, tell her.

Some things that often change with marriage include:

- Make-up: Some women wear it, some don't. A lot more women wear make-up, and wear it more frequently, when they are dating than they would if they were staying home alone with a close friend. Your husband is going to be your closest friend and you are going to spend a lot of time home alone with him. If you don't plan to wear make-up all the time once you're married, your partner should see you *au natural* before your marry. If you don't allow him to see you *au natural* before you marry, he should have the pleasure of always seeing you in make-up after you marry.
- Manners and social skills: Some men dress sharp, keep a spotless apartment, speak politely, open doors, stop to visit with parents, and generally act like a real gentlemen when

they're dating. Some of these men seem to lose all of these skills the day they get married. Not fair. Unless you plan to show your less refined side to your partner prior to marriage, you need to remain the gentleman for a lifetime, which, by the way, isn't a bad idea.

- Sex: Some women act like they can't get enough sex when they date and look forward to not having to have as much sex once they get married. Most men look forward to having sex more regularly once they get married. This causes problems! One young woman consulted with me complaining that her husband wouldn't keep his hands off her. I asked her if she had acted like she wanted sex all the time before they got married. Her response: "Of course! I didn't want to lose him." I told her I thought her husband has a right to expect her to continue to have sex all the time now that they're married, and I don't mean just for a few months, I mean forever.

- Romance: The other day, a friend at the gym asked me, "Why is it that guys seem to know exactly what you need them to do when you're dating and become clueless the minute you're married?" Lazy. Deceptive. Unfair. If romance was part of your dating strategy, it needs to be part of your marriage strategy as well.

We think trading faces is deceitful. We'd go so far as to call these behaviors lies. Trading faces definitely contributes to the disillusionment many couples experience upon marriage and undoubtedly contributes to the high divorce rate.

In business, it is illegal to offer one item for sale and then deliver a similar item of lesser quality. This tactic, referred to as bait and switch, is considered unethical and is generally done only by sleazy, fly by night operators. Where do you fall on this continuum? Are you reputable, or not?

Ultimately, divorce is a return of unsatisfactory merchandise. If you misrepresented the merchandise (you) that you planned to deliver to your partner in marriage, your partner is not going to be happy. If you change too much, your partner may return you for not being as advertised.

There is not one in a hundred of either sex, who is not taken in when they marry...It is, of all transactions, the one in which people expect most from others, and are least honest themselves.

Jane Austen, *Mansfield Park*

If you think it will be too difficult to keep up that false persona for the rest of your life, you might want to ask yourself the following questions.

Why did you do what you did?

For many of us, the answer is that we wanted our partner to like us or notice us. If you felt it was important to do this to make your partner like you during the short period of courtship, don't you think it's at least as important, to continue doing this now that you're together forever?

53

Did doing what you did while you were dating make your partner happier?

Yes? Think about it. You were willing to do this something to make a date happy. Remember, a date is a person you might never see again. Shouldn't you be more willing to do this same something to make your spouse happy? Your spouse has thrown his entire future in with you. Your spouse deserves your very best treatment.

Do you want your spouse to feel stuck with you?

I would certainly hope not. I feel blessed every day that Mike chooses to be married to me. It is a glorious feeling to know that he honestly would rather be with me than with anyone else. This is such a miracle! How did I get so lucky? I promise you, this is a much more positive feeling than I would have if I thought Mike felt stuck with a poor imitation of the person he dated.

What can you do in your marriage to make your spouse feel that she got a great deal when she married you?

Everything you did on your spouse's behalf while you dated was a mini-promise of what the future held if she would commit to be your wife. You owe it to each other to deliver the goods you promised.

This is a very simple trap to avoid. If you are married, be the person your spouse dated. If you are dating, be yourself.

You don't marry one person; you marry three:
the person you think they are,
the person they are, and
the person they are going to become
as the result of being married to you.

Richard Needham

I'm sorry. We're not open to the public.
Please choose from ready made stock on earth.

CLUE # 5

HE'S NOT
MR. POTATO HEAD®

D o you remember Mr. Potato Head®[1]? I loved creating various
characters by interchanging his eyes, ears, lips, teeth, legs, arms
and feet. Unfortunately, there were times when I tried to recreate a
guy I was dating with the same abandon that I rearranged Mr. Potato
Head®. I tried to rearrange his personality to suit me.

At some point it hit me that the problem was not with these
men. They didn't need to be saved, improved, molded or salvaged.
There was no turning Mr. Date into Mr. Right. They were already
right just the way they were. They just weren't right for me.

You can't make someone else change. Change comes from the
inside out. Someone must recognize the benefits of change and
choose to be different. The only person I can change is, was and
always will be me. And only you can change you, in case you haven't
picked that up.

It's truly amazing to me that any long-term relationship works

---

1 Mr. Potato Head® is a registered trademark of Hasbro, Inc.

when one considers the overwhelming urge to impose our will on others. It's so much easier to see how our partner could make a few little changes that would make our relationship better, rather than contemplating making comparable adjustments to oneself.

Things get even more convoluted when we marry. Once we're married, our partner is, to some extent, a reflection on, and of, us. Consequently, we unconsciously change the rules for our relationship. Make no mistake about it, our expectations of a spouse are different from those we had for a date, or even a live-in lover.

Whether you're aware of it or not, each of us has been formulating since childhood a concept of the ideal spouse. These images combine attributes observed through personal contact, television, movies, books, newspapers and other media, blended with a good dash of imagination.

Today, consider changing yourself rather than someone else. Sometimes the effect is the same.

Source Unknown

Although you may never have given it conscious thought, you know how your ideal spouse would treat you, talk to you when you're down, handle your birthday, relate to your parents, interact with your friends and dress.

Even if you can't describe these in detail without prompting, you intuitively know how he'd act in every circumstance. Walk into a restaurant and look at the patrons. You'll automatically judge who is dressed properly, whose table manners are appropriate, who's acting the right way. Go anywhere and watch any couple; you know when one of the partners does something right or wrong.

Can you see how easy it is to end up marrying an image? This is another reason why so many couples end up disillusioned as time goes by. You may fall into the trap of trying to change your partner to match your ideal. If you're not aware of what's going on and aren't actively working to avoid it, you almost can't help yourself.

No partner will hold up well over time if constantly compared to your ideal image. Your partner isn't privy to your imagination, so she has no way of knowing what's expected of her. To add to the problem, what you're expecting keeps changing as your ideal image evolves through time.

When you find yourself wanting to change your partner, remember, this is YOUR preconception so it's yours to change. Consider going with your partner as is. You'll both be a lot happier with this attitude. We suggest you replace your images with something that will work better for you, a realistic profile of your partner. In Part III of this book, we'll lead you through a simple process that will allow each of you to clearly see the person your spouse is. It's a wonderful and exciting opportunity to learn more about each other.

As you examine your partner's realistic profile, there's nothing wrong with noting where her actual traits differ from what you had expected, just resist the urge to change them. Over time, you will find that many of the ways your partner deviates from what you expected will just be a point of difference, while other differences will actually be better than the trait you hoped for. One unexpected treasure I discovered in Mike is the way he puts me on a pedestal. I always expected to be treated as an equal, but I must say I'm rather fond of the view from up here!

*In my house I'm the boss,
my wife is just the decision maker.*

Woody Allen

CLUE # 6

WHY I ALWAYS
GET MY WAY

In our marriage, we almost always do things my way on a day to day basis. If you're expecting a punch line for this secret, there isn't one. This is not a joke. Mike actually offered this to me early in our discussions. Why? Because Mike really doesn't care about most things, so it's easier for him to abdicate routine decisions to me.

If you think it's silly to bother with an agreement about something like this, think again. The decision maker tends to have power in a relationship. Consequently, making decisions can become a power struggle for many couples – even when one or both of them don't care about the outcome of the decision. People get wrapped up in having things done their way just because they don't want to give up their power.

If you have never openly discussed how you will reach decisions in your relationship, you'll find that coming to an agreement now on how you will make future decisions may eliminate power struggles in your relationship. This will save you time, reduce misunderstandings and minimize hurt feelings.

---

*Nearly all men can stand adversity,
but if you want to test a man's character,
give him power.*

Abraham Lincoln

Give one person power and he becomes a dictator, another wants to be treated like royalty in his own private kingdom and yet another creates a democracy.

- In a marriage dictatorship, one partner makes all the decisions and implements them without consideration of the other's wishes or needs.
- In a kingdom, one person sits on a pedestal and directs the other person to serve her; her authority comes from having been put on the pedestal by a willing subject (her spouse).
- In a democracy, both partners have equal power and share decision making and enforcement.

While every relationship includes a touch of each of these attributes from time to time, most couples tend to operate most often under one of the above formats. While there really isn't one form of power structure that's right for every marriage, it is important that you know which role you're agreeing to play in your relationship. A marriage between two dictators will become a battleground.

Operating a democracy in marriage is much more difficult than running a democratic country. Democracy hinges on the wishes of the majority. With a marriage, there are only two people, so the only way to attain a majority is to find a solution you can unanimously support. This can be very difficult.

Mike and I operate under a benevolent dictatorship on a day to day basis and a democracy when it comes to major decisions. I call my dictatorship benevolent because Mike gave me my dictatorial powers. I didn't take Mike's power away from him. If you end up fighting over silly little things, you might want to consider creating a dictatorship, as we did.

Here's how we work things. I am one of those people who care about everything. Big things, little things, tiny details; everything matters to me. Mike, at the other extreme, doesn't care about many things at all and doesn't want to be bothered with details. As a result, I make all of our day to day decisions. When Mike cares about a particular issue, it's up to him to let me know.

---

*Live so that when your children think of fairness,
caring and integrity, they think of you.*

H. Jackson Browne, Jr

When Mike tells me he cares about something, I know that he cares passionately about it. Generally, in those circumstances, we do things his way because, while I care about virtually everything, I don't care about many things at a passionate level.

When both of us care passionately about something and our opinions differ, we keep talking until we understand why each of us feels the way we do. We both start out equally entitled to our opinions. He gets no credit for letting me have my way most of the time. Usually, the right thing to do becomes pretty clear once everything is out in the open. I'm not saying we're both delighted with what the right thing turns out to be, but we agree to do it cheerfully anyway.

For example, the decision to sell the dream home that we built and move into a much smaller apartment was not an easy one to reach. I loved the house, the yard, the neighborhood, my friends, my stuff in the house, everything. Mike liked many of the attributes of the house, but all the stuff was making him feel claustrophobic. Additionally, he felt the house owned all of our free time, energy and disposable income. To him, the house was somewhere between an albatross and a nightmare.

We discussed selling the house many times. Over a four year period, our discussions would end with Mike deciding that my love of the house was greater than his discomfort, and we should keep the house. As interim solutions, we sold and donated things from the house to make the environment more comfortable for Mike.

Eventually, it became clear that the house was winning its emotional battle with Mike. He seemed really sad and down much of the time and, occasionally, downright angry. Mike was not happy and wasn't able to maintain a grin and bear it attitude any longer. At this point, the right thing to do was to sell the house. We sold the house. Ultimately, the house was just a place to live. It wasn't nearly as important as Mike's happiness and mental health.

Please don't think that all of our conversations remain rational and unemotional. I promise you that Mike yelled occasionally as he expressed his frustration with the house. I cried uncontrollably at times thinking of all the things I'd be giving up if we sold the house.

What helped us keep things in perspective is that our emotions were always directed at the house and not at each other. This may seem like a fine point, but it made a big difference. I never felt that Mike didn't want me to be happy and I hope he never felt that way about my wishes for him. It really was about our personal relationships with the house. We both knew that the relationship between the two of us was more important to each of us than the house was.

How do you know if something is more important to you than your relationship? Ask yourself a "What would I choose?" question. Here's an example of what I asked myself about our house. "If I were forced to choose between living in this house alone and never seeing Mike again, or living with Mike someplace else, where would I want to live?"

When you create a "What would you choose?" question, the choices must be black and white; no hybrid solutions allowed. In this case, my choices were 'house' or 'Mike.' Put this way, it was very easy to choose to sell the house.

---

*Every man must find his own philosophy...
his attitude toward life.*

Lin Yutang

Mike loves to tell people that I always get my way in our marriage. He thinks it's funny when others get tied up in knots over the way we structure our marriage. No matter how you structure your relationship, there will always be someone out there who will think your rules are ridiculous or unreasonable. Ignore outside opinions. What works for the two of you is the only thing that matters.

The greatest griefs are those we cause ourselves.

Sophocles

If you are both people who care about all the details, you might decide to alternate days, weeks or months during which each of you get your way. Our daughter Andi and her husband Wendell primarily operate as a democracy, but when they can't come to an agreement he has the final say on everything. They have been happily married six years.

My grandmother was a total princess and my grandfather seemed to love waiting on her hand and foot. When anyone criticized my grandmother for bossing my grandfather around, my grandfather was quick to come to her defense saying that he did everything for her out of love. They were happily married more than 50 years.

Another couple we know makes no pretense that the wife has any input on anything – he is a total dictator. You can hear my judgment in that description – such an arrangement would never work for me. They, on the other hand, seem to work well with this agreement and have been happily married 35 years.

Do not come to this agreement lightly. Remember, you are committing to operate this way for the rest of your life. You will not have the power to unilaterally decide you don't like the arrangement anymore and change it. You might be able to renegotiate your power structure, then again, you might not. Remember, few people want to give up power once they have it.

Our personalities dictated our distribution of power. If your balance of power is less clear, decide on a trial period to try out a number of different decision making arrangements. It seems likely that one of these will seem most comfortable to you.

If you are able to come to an agreement with your spouse on the way you will structure your marriage, it will make it much easier for you to reach your milestone anniversaries and still be happy and in love.

Where love rules, there is no will to power;
and where power predominates, there love is lacking.
The one is the shadow of the other.

Carl Jung

My wife's lack of desire has created tension between us. If I press the issue and she still doesn't want to have sex, then she feels bad for saying no, and I feel bad for forcing the issue. So over time you quit touching as much because it might lead to that awkward moment.

Joe Kita, in *Men's Health*

NEVER SAY NO
TO SEX

No, we don't mean you should say "Yes" to anyone! Just your spouse.

Whether to have sex before you are married is a highly sensitive and emotionally charged personal decision. I grew up in the sexually liberated seventies when celibacy was considered passé. In retrospect, I am appalled at how little thought I gave to my personal choices. I can tell you that for me, sex as a single wasn't liberating, fulfilling or meaningful. In fact, I came to the rather unsettling realization that the average prostitute had more integrity in her sexual relationships than I had. At least with a prostitute, both parties know why they are having sex.

I was using sex to reward, punish and manipulate. All the wrong reasons. As I talked with other sexually active singles, I found that virtually all of them were having sex for all the wrong reasons as well. In addition to my rationale, I heard the following:

- to keep him interested

- to make someone love me
- it's expected
- everyone does it
- to ultimately get what I want
- to avoid talking about things
- to prove my desirability
- to be cool, with it, au current
- to fill the emptiness

In talking with married individuals, they admitted using sex for many of the above reasons, as well. With so many ulterior motives, it's no wonder that sex frequently becomes a battleground in marriage.

When Mike and I decided to get married, I didn't want sex to become a problem, so I suggested to Mike that we never say "No" when the other person wanted sex. After three or four seconds of deep contemplation, he caved and said, "Okay, we'll do it your way." We have lived by this philosophy for nearly 25 years and we both feel it has been one of our happiest agreements.

We feel that never saying no is SMART because it:

S	Stops
M	Manipulation
A	And
R	Removes
T	Temptation

- It is SMART to address your genuine grievances outside the bedroom.
- It is SMART to have sex for the right reasons – mutual pleasure, as well as procreation.
- It is SMART to recognize that a refusal to have sex over an extended period of time is going to make temptation that much more attractive to your partner.

I'm not saying it's right to stray, but we all know it happens – and happens frequently. The issue of fidelity is something we believe every couple should discuss. Questions included in Part V, The Marriage Pact™ Questionnaire, will help you express your opinions on this issue and guide you through a conversation.

When Mike and I discussed the issue of fidelity before we married, Mike promised that he would never go elsewhere for sex as long as he got sex at home, but he did not plan to go without sex. This brought on discussions of, "What if I were paralyzed, or critically ill, or amputated from the waist down and on a feeding tube?"

Our bottom line was that physical limitations would not prompt infidelity, manipulatively withholding sex might. Since infidelity would most likely end our marriage, this was an extremely important conversation for us to have before we married.

---

*The way to love anything
is to realize that it might be lost.*

G. K. Chesterton

We have shared our never say no to sex philosophy with other couples and it has transformed the relationships of those who implemented it. It has been so successful, that we would recommend that every couple put this into practice. We really don't think there is any other reasonable choice. Think about it. If you are going to be selective about when you will have sex and when you won't, then sex is very likely to become a bargaining chip or an act of manipulation rather than a display of love and affection.

And what about when you really don't feel like it? Our secret is that while we always say "Yes" for our spouse, we can say "No" for ourselves. In other words, you don't have to become mentally, emotionally and sexually involved, you merely have to please your spouse.

You will need to determine your personal rules for sex within which the 'never say no' rule is applied. As you create your Marriage Pact in Part III of this book, you'll have an opportunity to discuss if and how you see a never say no to sex policy working in your marriage. Here is how it works for us.

First of all, there is the practical matter of timing. If we were walking through a park when the urge hit one of us, we would not rush into the bushes to make love. Nor, if we were in a restaurant, would we escape to the coat closet for a quickie. Hey, if that works for you, that's up to you, but for us, if one of us wants sex, that person has to wait until common sense and decency laws allow - although we may have pushed the law to the limit on occasion. For us, looking forward to an interlude heightens the pleasure of the ultimate event. We generally have sex at home or where we are spending the night.

It doesn't matter what you do in the bedroom as long as you don't do it in the street and frighten the horses

Mrs. Patrick Campbell

Then, there is the matter of approach. If one of us wants sex, that person makes whatever overture feels right at the time: a touch, a suggestive word or an out-and-out proposal. If the other person is genuinely interested, things progress on their own. If the other person doesn't want sex, rather than pretending he isn't getting the message, feigning sleep or whatever, he acknowledges the other person's desire and his lack of it by saying something to the effect of, "Would you like me to service you?" This is said pleasantly and playfully and lets the other person know that he is more than willing to satisfy her.

We've both had experience saying this and, over the years, we've gotten quite good at making servicing sound as terrific as it is. If one of us is already asleep and the other comes to bed feeling frisky, he (or she) wakes up the sleeping party and says something like, "Sorry honey, I really need you to service me."

Our rule is that the person who doesn't want to have sex gets to pick the location, style, position and whatever other details there may be. That person's only obligation is to satisfy the other person's needs. The uninterested party does not have to do any specific anything as long as the mission is accomplished.

Of course, one of us can always ask for special favors, but the other person has no obligation to deliver. Generally, however, if one of us wants something specific, the other is happy to comply. After all, the point is to make your partner happy, and if a particular something will make Mike happy, what difference does it make to me?

For those of you who feel that this sounds cold and can't imagine having your partner 'service' you, would you rather do without? Some people might. We wanted to be realistic. We knew plenty of couples who complained about the lack of sex in their marriage, even after a vigorous sex life prior to marriage. Sex was a huge problem in those marriages, in some cases leading to infidelity, in others divorce. We wanted to address differing levels of sex drive because every couple faces this sooner or later. I had several women friends who had gone for extended periods without sex in their marriages, and I didn't want that for me.

We've often been asked if performing on demand makes our relationship mechanical or sterile. The answer is no. I personally think our agreement is highly erotic. What more intimate way is there for us to demonstrate our love for the other than giving pleasure when one's not in the mood? After all, there's no sacrifice being made when you both want sex!

When I am being serviced, I am in seventh heaven. I don't have to worry about feeling selfish, which can be a real problem for me. Sometimes during 'regular' sex that little voice in the back of my head will absolutely drive me crazy, "You're not giving enough." "You're almost comatose, you'd better snap out of it and make sure he's having a great time, too."

On one level I know this is ridiculous, but on another level I can't help myself. When I'm being serviced, I can focus completely on me. It's great.

For those of you concerned that servicing will become a way of life, I guess you have to look at your relationship and your relative sex drives. For us, historically, it's probably 80% regular sex and 20% servicing, but that definitely depends on the year. I went through eight years of clinical depression and I had virtually no interest in sex during all of that time. During those years, 100% of our sex started with me servicing Mike. Fortunately, once you get started, the uninterested party frequently becomes very interested. What begins as servicing often doesn't end up that way.

Lest you think the servicing always goes one way, it doesn't. It goes in phases. We believe our approach is an honest and direct way to handle the peaks and valleys that any two people might experience while still ensuring that both their needs are met.

Do you HAVE to adopt a never say no approach to sex to have a fabulous relationship? Of course not. But you DO have to be in agreement as to what you will do when one of you wants sex and the other doesn't.

Marriage: the state or condition of a community consisting of a master, a mistress and two slaves, making in all two.

Ambrose Bierce

A final word of caution; requesting sex should be done in the same spirit of love as the giving of sex when you don't totally feel like it. Initiating sex at inappropriate moments can be just as manipulative as saying "No" to punish someone.

Avoid using sex for ulterior motives, for example, to:
- end a discussion or win an argument
- avoid talking about something
- make your spouse prove his love for you by choosing between you and a business or social commitment
- demean your partner or display your power over her

Never saying "No" to each other has worked very well for us and we would encourage you to give it a try...say for 25 years!

Second-guessing your spouse's preferences can
make your relationship second rate.

LET ME MAKE THIS PERFECTLY CLEAR

Has your partner ever reacted totally inappropriately when you've been upset?

- You want to be left alone and she's trying to comfort you?
- You need to talk with someone and he takes one look at you and disappears into the bathroom with a book?

Have you ever wondered if you were speaking some foreign language because your spouse doesn't understand your needs? Guess what? Your partner wants to be part of the things in your life that make you happy, but he is a victim of a "Catch 22." How can your partner make you happy when only you know what will please you at any given moment?

It is your job to let your partner know how to make you happy in a particular situation. Tell your partner what you want. Be satisfied when he gives you what you asked for. If you can keep communications this uncomplicated, it will greatly simplify your relationship and I think you'll be impressed with how easy it is to talk with each other.

Unfortunately, most people don't make communicating easy. They assume their partner will be on the same wave length, will know how they feel at a given moment and will know what they want them to do. This is just about impossible. We are often inconsistent. And while unpredictability is one of the things that can make us unique, fascinating and appealing, it can also make pleasing us very frustrating. For instance, sometimes when I'm upset I want to be left alone, occasionally I want to talk, other times I want to be held. How is Mike supposed to know what I expect from him when I am upset if I don't tell him?

It's best to ask for what you need from your loved ones and not assume that somehow they will just know.

Source Unknown

When you want a specific response from your partner, preface your conversation with a statement that identifies how you're feeling and tells her what you want from her:

"I feel lousy. I need a hug."

"I feel lousy. I want to be left alone."

"I feel lousy. I want to talk while you comfort me, but I don't want any input."

If this sounds a bit simplistic, you are right. It's very simple. And it works. Not only can it keep you from getting into trouble, but if you do get into trouble, it can help get you out. Here's a real life example:

CLUE #8: LET ME MAKE THIS PERFECTLY CLEAR

My mom was visiting us when she learned that her sister had breast cancer. For two days she carried on as if nothing was going on. Finally, the reality hit her and she fell apart, sobbing. What she wanted was to be comforted by my dad. Unfortunately, while it was 11 PM where we were, it was 2 AM on the east coast where he was. She called him anyway, but the conversation was not soothing and reassuring. In fact it became a loud example of miscommunication.

Jolted by the middle of the night call, Dad expected someone to be dead. With his adrenaline flowing, he demanded to know why she had to call in the middle of the night when she had already waited two days to tell him. She was defensive and tried to justify her actions.

I slipped a note in front of her, "Tell him you're very upset and you need his support." She pushed the note away and proceeded to try to explain her situation. The conversation was escalating into an argument. Finally she said, "Well, I just called because I needed your support." Things immediately simmered down. When she got off the phone she said, "Thank you. Even your father couldn't resist an appeal for his support, but I hate playing games like that."

I believe she would have gotten the comfort and support she craved from his opening words had she started out by saying, "Phil, I'm very upset and I need your support." Our contention is that telling someone exactly what you want is not game playing. Quite the opposite! Game playing is making someone guess what you want and what it will take to make you happy.

Don't set each other up for failure. Ensure success. It's your job to be specific. Don't expect that anyone can guess your needs. They're your needs and they will change frequently. Keep your partner updated.

"I had a terrible day at work, would you please leave me alone for fifteen minutes so I can fall apart."

"I had the best day! Be happy for me!"

"I'm feeling sorry for myself and I just want you to listen while I complain."

"I'm really mad at Nancy. I want you to agree with me."

When sensitive issues come up, preparing your partner will preempt misunderstandings.

"I need to talk, but my feelings are so mixed up I'm sure everything's going to get jumbled up. I just want you to listen and not get upset because I know this isn't going to come out right."

Need a reward? Don't hesitate to tell your partner!

"I'm proud of myself. I fixed that faucet you've been reminding me about since last May. I could use a hug and a glass of lemonade."

Being specific will not only give you the best chance of getting you what you want, but it will also give your partner the confidence of knowing she's done exactly the right thing. You both win.

Communicate completely. Give up any hidden agendas. When you ask for something, your partner has the right to expect you to be happy when you get it. Clinging to hidden agendas is a huge problem for many couples.

If you're too beat to cook and ask your partner to pick up something for dinner on his way home from work, be satisfied with anything he selects. It's not his job to remember that six nights ago when you were at a sushi bar you mentioned, "Boy, this is my idea of a great carry out meal." If you want sushi, say so.

And if you say "Pick up a pizza," don't go feeling cheated if you get a medium when you wanted an extra large, or if the pizza came from Little Italy and you wanted the house special from Tony's.

There's nothing wrong with wanting things done your way, but it's not fair to expect someone else to know what your way is today. If the details matter, be specific.

Some people say that what's not said is just as important as what is said. If you want to have a terrific relationship, don't make that true for you. Don't make your partner guess what's going on in your mind.

It is equally important that you accept what is said at face value. Don't read between the lines. If your partner says he had a bad day at work and wants to be left alone, believe it. Don't assume he's still brooding over harsh words you had yesterday.

It's your partner's job to tell you what he's thinking and what he wants from you. It's your job to believe it and do your best to deliver what is wanted.

People don't get married because they want to irritate each other. They get married because they need each other and want to make each other happy. When you love someone, you are willing to do almost anything for her as long as you know it's what she wants you to do. This is true for you. It's also true for your partner. If you find yourself being irritated, identify what's going wrong and talk to your partner. She doesn't want to be a thorn in your side; give her the courtesy of letting her know exactly what it will take to make you happy.

If you remember that your partner wants to be part of the things in your life that make you happy, it will make it easier to communicate effectively. When each of you say what you mean and mean what you say, you'll find that you both will get more of what you want much more often in your marriage. Now, won't that make you happier?

There's a difference between
upholding the letter of the law and
maintaining the spirit of your agreements.

IS IT WORTH IT?

Have you ever found yourself mired in an escalating battle of wills? How did it make you feel? If you have a limited amount of time to spend with your spouse, is this how you want to spend it?

Don't think I'm asking you to sanitize your marriage into "yes, dear" mediocrity. Please don't act like a couple of bobble heads agreeing with whatever the other says. But it is helpful to assess your tolerance for discord as a couple.

The first step in doing this is to honestly ask yourselves how much each of you enjoys a healthy debate. Mike and I are a study of contrasts. Mike really enjoys locking horns with anyone on any topic. He is fascinated with the art of persuasion. He has been known to switch sides in the middle of a debate and manipulate his opponent into arguing his case for him. For Mike, verbal sparring is an invigorating way to spend time with friend or foe.

I, at the other extreme, am not nearly as confrontational. Much of what Mike perceives as healthy debate, I perceive as fighting.

Flaring tempers and raised voices aren't fun to me. I am interested in what other people think, I enjoy sharing perspectives, but I generally don't care if others feel the way I do. If you want to be happily married, your tolerance for discord as a couple is only as great as the less aggressive spouse's. Mike has a number of favorite sparring partners, but I am not one of them.

It may be helpful for you to identify topics that you will not discuss. These could be areas where you agree to disagree or they could be topics that are too emotional to confront except when absolutely necessary. We have a number of hot topics we've agreed not to discuss. On a couple of these topics we vehemently agree - yes you read that correctly. We both end up so wound up when we discuss them that I am an emotional wreck for the rest of the day. This isn't how we want to spend our time together, so we just don't go there.

The last fight was my fault.
-My wife asked, "What's on the TV?"
I said, "Dust."

Red Skelton

We believe if you're going to have conflict, it should be worth the time and energy you invest in it. To help us decide if a battle is worthwhile, we ask ourselves the following questions:

1. Can I solve the problem?

   If neither of us is a party to the problem and we don't

have the power to solve the problem, we won't waste energy arguing about it. This eliminates getting involved in the disagreements of friends and relatives, as well as, global issues. We can not personally stop world hunger or restore the ozone layer, so while we may support groups working on these issues and we try to live responsibly, we aren't going to argue about them.

2. Will the outcome be significant in five years?

If the outcome of the situation will not be important in five years, how much time and attention does it really warrant today? This actually eliminates most disagreements.

3. What is the disagreement REALLY about?

Nothing gets resolved if you're not addressing the real problem. A conflict about where to go for dinner is rarely about food. The real issue could be one of these:

- Finances – we really can't afford to eat out.
- Personal responsibility – you said you'd do the cooking, so where's dinner?
- Respect – we always go out for pizza, why don't I ever get to decide where we go?

Once Mike and I agreed that if we're going to have conflict it must be worth the time and energy we invest in it, it was amazing to see how little there was to disagree about. Most issues just aren't worth the effort.

Try using these questions and they will quickly become second nature to you. Sometimes I'll hear that little voice in the back of my head saying, "it's not going to matter in five years, just let it go" and I won't even have been aware that I was getting drawn into something. Using these questions as quick screening tools will save you a lot of time and wasted emotions in your marriage and in your other relationships, as well.

Too many people spend money they haven't earned,
to buy things they don't want,
to impress people they don't like.

Will Smith

MONEY MATTERS

As unromantic as it sounds, the financial side of marriage is a business. For those of you who hate math, are diametrically opposed to business or think that economics belongs in a classroom, get over it. Marriage is business, big business. In the course of your marriage, you will handle hundreds of thousands, perhaps millions, of dollars. The sooner you take responsibility for the financial health of your marriage, the better off you'll be.

There is nothing innately difficult about running the financial side of a relationship, provided that you are both on the same page. Our objective is to help you get on the same page. To us, being on the same page means having the same spending philosophy, financial goals and spending priorities.

When Mike asked me to marry him, he told me not to accept if I had an attachment to any material thing I owned. It was his dream to start his own business and he was willing to risk everything he had to make it work. Additionally, he had been married previously and paid his ex-wife $850 a month child support. Remember, this was twenty-five years ago so this was BIG money for us. Since this obligation preceded any commitment to me, I needed to agree that we would meet this financial commitment before we spent any money on anything for us, including food. I agreed, fully expecting that our new business venture would make us millionaires.

I had demands, too. I was only willing to get married if we operated on a "cash" basis. To me this meant we would pay cash for everything except our home or a major investment. Mike had previously financed his cars – a concept that was totally unacceptable to me. If Mike married me, we would not purchase a car or anything else until we could pay cash for it. Mike agreed, fully expecting that, as future millionaires, this wasn't going to mean doing without anything.

Mike and I were on the same page when we married:
- spending philosophy: pay cash; use credit only to buy a house or investments
- financial goals: become self-employed millionaires
- spending priorities: #1 child support, #2 food and housing, #3 savings, #4 everything else

As you know by now, our real estate development business failed. If you think that failure made being on the same page immaterial, you're missing the point. Being on the same page made our financial fall orderly and unemotional. I hope you never have to go through similarly difficult times, but if you do, being on the same page will remove anger and uncertainty from the equation.

So, how can you establish a spending philosophy, financial goals and spending priorities? I think the best way to start is to answer the following question: Do you want to look like you have money or do you actually want to have money? If you and your spouse can agree on an answer to this question, it will become easier to make financial decisions that move you towards your goal.

If you just care about looking like you have money, you're probably already doing what you need to do: loading up those credit cards, buying your favorite status symbols and living beyond your means. On the surface, this is the easy road to follow because it takes no discipline and it provides instant gratification.

Unfortunately, for most couples, it is ultimately very stressful. Inevitably, one of you is left to deal with creditors calling and financed items being repossessed. Most of us have a low tolerance for the inconvenience of being hounded by collection agents or the humiliation of the local grocery store refusing to accept our checks. If you are not okay with the long term implications of this approach, poor credit and possible bankruptcy, your spending habits are bound to become a divisive force in your marriage.

Money often costs too much.

Ralph Waldo Emerson

On the other hand, if you actually want to have money, chances are you will go for a number of years looking like you don't have much money. This not only takes self discipline, it takes a great deal of self esteem because there are bound to be others talking about their plasma TV, new car, remodeled kitchen, exotic vacation or whatever. So, without being smug, you do need to be well grounded in your dedication to becoming financially secure.

The secret to having money is paying your credit card balance in full every month, saving a portion of every paycheck and making investments. The goal most often recommended is that you save 10% of your income. The most painless way to do this is to have your employer direct deposit 10% of each paycheck into your savings account. If that option is not available, it will take a bit more discipline, but it's worth it. Every time you receive money, put 10% of it into a savings account and leave it there. When money is tight, it may seem impossible to live on less money. But almost no matter what your income, there are people who make 10% less than you do who get by. You should build up a rainy day fund of several months' income and the rest of the money should be invested.

This means doing without some of those status symbols you want today. It doesn't mean you never get to have the toys; it just means you wait a few years until you have attained certain financial goals before you buy them. When you do buy them, you pay cash out of your earnings from your investments.

One thing that helps me curb my spending is asking, "Will I still want to be paying for this item fifty years from now?" I heard on the radio not too long ago that if you're making the minimum payment on your credit card, it will take you more than 50 years to pay off an item. I can't think of a meal I've eaten or an item I've purchased that I'll even remember in 50 years, so I definitely don't want to still be making payments on it. Using this screening question helps me put the brakes on my spending and keep the amount we charge in the range that we can pay off in full each month.

People have repeatedly asked us how we lived on so little after our business failed. We went from a combined income of over $90,000 in 1980 to an average combined income of less than $7,000 for the first seven years of our marriage. The secret is simple.

*Rethink your buying habits.
Try to come up with a creative solution
rather than buying a solution to a perceived need.*

Simplify Your Life, daily calendar

We gave up day to day luxuries like cable TV, special service packs on our telephone, cell phones, a second car, new clothes, eating out, snack foods, fresh produce out of season, deli and bakery items, brand name foods, movies and other forms of paid entertainment. We made a game out of seeing how little money we could spend on groceries for a week. We lived in a mobile home. When we couldn't afford the luxury of a mobile home, we camped out of our car, but we never carried a balance on our credit cards.

These were serious lifestyle changes for us, but we didn't have the money for a "better" lifestyle. In retrospect, we were as happy then as we have ever been in our lives. We enjoyed each other's company. We hiked for miles delighted by the amazing Colorado scenery. We took picnic outings to collect deadfall wood for our wood stove to save on heating costs. It truly wasn't a hardship. It was heady to experience each other's commitment to living within our means.

The wisdom we learned during our lean years has stayed with us and impacts our frugality today. Here are some of the cost-cutting measures we've retained:

You don't really pay for things with money. You pay for them with time. "In five years, I'll have put enough away to buy that vacation house we want. Then I'll slow down." That means the house will cost you five years -- one-twelfth of your adult life. Translate the dollar value of the house, car or anything else into time, and then see if it's still worth it. Sometimes you can't do what you want and have what you want at once because each requires a different expenditure of time. The phrase "spending your time" is not a metaphor. It's how life works..

Dr. Charles Spezzano, *What to Do Between Birth and Death*

- buy used cars to avoid the drastic depreciation in the first year
- own one car - rent a second car when one is needed
- use public transportation when possible
- eat out as a special treat, not as a way of life
- reasonable number of clothes in our closets
- reasonable gift giving
- basic cable (local reception is unacceptable without it)
- prepaid cell phone used exclusively for important calls
- limited frills on our telephone

Are we this frugal in all areas? No, but we remain on the same page when it comes to financial issues, although you'll note that our goals and priorities have changed through the years:

- spending philosophy: pay cash; use credit only to buy a house or other real estate
- financial goals: be self-employed and able to afford retirement
- spending priorities: #1 retirement savings, #2 food and housing, #3 philanthropy, #4 everything else

We encourage you to sit down with your spouse and agree on an overall spending philosophy, set financial goals and designate your spending priorities. Write down your agreements and post them on the bathroom mirror, refrigerator or some other prominent place.

Your household is a miniature economy. The success of this economic venture is totally up to you. The more successful you are in spending in accordance with your financial philosophy, the happier you are likely to be.

*A soul mate isn't something you find;
a soul mate is someone you intentionally
and prayerfully become.*

Tim Alan Gardner

Clue # 11

CALMING CUES

We've all known couples who drive each other crazy by rehashing the same problems over and over again. Anytime you think, "Here they go again," you're probably reacting to a drama that everyone would love to eliminate. Unfortunately, many couples lack the skills to stop auto-replay from cycling endlessly.

We've come up with what we call our "calming cues." This is a secret language we use when we feel ourselves falling into bad habits that have traditionally had us going at it. I hope this doesn't disillusion you – everyone has problems – it's how you choose to cope with them that determines whether you'll be happily married or not.

Now there's good news and bad news about our calming cues. The good news is that you probably don't have these exact problems in your relationship. The bad news is that since you don't have these exact problems, our solutions won't be directly applicable to you. I think you'll get enough of a drift from these examples that you can apply a similar approach in your marriage.

Sometimes I'll sense a change in the tone of Mike's voice which means there is a very strong probability that he's about to start picking on someone, usually me. Rather than let things escalate, I'll say, "I hear Mr. Mister!" When Mike hears the words "Mr. Mister," he takes a deep breath and changes gears. I can tell by watching his face that this transition is extremely difficult for him, but he does a great job of curtailing his comments and changing his attitude.

Trigger: Change in tone of voice

Phrase: I hear Mr. Mister

Action: Stop picking on whomever (especially if it's me!) and change the subject

---

Managing your emotions is an inside job.
That's why it's important to learn techniques
to make attitude adjustments.
You can then direct your emotions more efficiently.
Happiness comes through emotions qualified by the heart.

Doc Childre and Howard Martin, *The HeartMath Solution*

Mike has very sensitive toes and my size ten shoes manage to tread on his size fourteen's with uncanny regularity. In considerable pain, he used to give me a thorough tongue-lashing. One time when I stepped on his foot, he stood glaring at me, searching for the right zinger to tell me how clumsy I am. I blurted out, "I think that meant that I need a hug." Mike snickered and said, "Oh, excuse me, I must have misunderstood." After a bit of banter, he finally gave me a hug and a new meaning was given to the act of my treading on his toes. Now when I step on Mike's toes, he winces and then I say, "I guess I need a hug." We hug.

    Trigger: Me stepping on Mike's toes

    Phrase: I guess I need a hug.

    Action: We hug

Sometimes I'll micromanage Mike's day to day activities to the point that it feels condescending to him: Do you need help with this? Let me get that for you. Did you know your car door's open? He'll tolerate my over-helpfulness to a point and then it will really start getting on his nerves. When he's had enough, instead of exploding he'll ask me in a playful tone, "Do you think I'm so stupid that I don't know my car door is open?" We don't remember how this phrase started but it makes us laugh. It's a great reminder that he needs a little more space and I'll back off.

    Trigger: Me being over-helpful on too many things

    Phrase: Do you think I'm so stupid that...?

    Action: Back off. Leave him alone.

Calming cues are one of the ways Mike and I regularly demonstrate kindness to each other. It is kind to help your partner avoid behavior that he will later regret. It is kind to accept a gentle nudge and avoid hurtful behavior.

Kindness is the life's blood, the elixir of marriage. Kindness makes the difference between passion and caring. Kindness is tenderness. Kindness is love, but perhaps greater than love ... Kindness is good will. Kindness says, "I want you to be happy." Kindness comes very close to the benevolence of God.

Randolph Ray in *My Little Church around the Corner*

Well enough about us. What about you? Much of your happiness boils down to your perception of things. You choose your perceptions, so it's in your power to be happy in your relationship. As always, simple truths sound overly simplistic, but they work.

Here's how you can create your secret language of calming cues.

- First off, identify specific triggers that one of you recognizes as starting the auto-replay sequence.
- Assign a designated word or phrase to correspond with each unique trigger. Only the two of you know the exact meaning of this word or phrase, but in essence it's going to mean, "Oops. We're headed down the wrong path. Let's not go there."
- Agree what action should be taken by each of you once this

phrase has been said. We've agreed that the universally appropriate response for the person who says the phrase is to back off and not say anything else. This gives the person who has to change gears a few seconds of quiet to mentally refocus and make the changes needed.

Your secret language can be used in response to both verbal and physical triggers. When one of your triggers pops up in your day to day life, you say the word or phrase that you've assigned to that particular trigger. When your partner hears the words from your secret language, she changes gears and acts appropriately based on the response you agreed to follow when developing your calming cues.

Having calming cues doesn't eliminate the problem – the triggers will still occur. I still accidentally step on Mike's toes and his toes still hurt when I step on them. I'm still overly helpful and Mike still starts to sound nasty. What has changed is the way we react to these repetitious circumstances. The calming cues give you a chance to change the course of events that follow and prevent the incident from escalating into an uncomfortable situation or conflict. They give you a chance to change confrontation into kindness.

It's often the little things that sabotage happiness. You have the ability to turn those unpleasantries to your advantage. Do it.

The most powerful agent of growth and transformation is something much more basic than any technique: a change of heart.

John Welwood

BONUS VIEWPOINT –
NO EXTRA CHARGE

Calming cues aren't just for interactions with your partner, they are also a great way to salve your hurt pride and quiet that little voice inside your head that judges your actions. We are frequently our harshest critics. Have you ever embarrassed yourself by tripping, dropping or running into something? I certainly have, and more than once my internal response was something like, "How could I be so clumsy?"

At some point in high school or college, I read that your subconscious mind likes to provide answers to these questions. So when you leave yourself with an open-ended question like, "How could I be so clumsy?" or "Could I do anything dumber?" your subconscious mind gets to work and you start discovering the answers through your actions.

- Here's a way I can be so clumsy.
- Here's another way I can be so clumsy.
- Yes, I can do something dumber, and I just did.
- Here's another dumber thing. Wow. I can do lots of dumber things.

The way to put your subconscious mind to work for you is to replace the critical open ended questions with a positive statement. Various statements I have used include:

- I will be more careful next time.
- I won't make that mistake again.
- I do smart things.

None of these responses felt comfortable to me. Additionally, my cynical mind would play with me and say things like, "You may not make that mistake, but you'll make others." I was defeating my own positive reinforcement.

Ultimately I came up with a statement which has become my hallmark. "Well, that wasn't my first choice." This is the first thing out of my mouth when I trip, run into something or do something dim-witted. The first time Mike heard me use it I had just dropped a bowl of still liquid cherry Jell-O® [1] all over the interior of the refrigerator, the floor and myself. He stood in awe as I said, "Well, that certainly wasn't my first choice!" started giggling and got on with the job of cleaning up.

I have found that saying, "Well, that wasn't my first choice" is not only calming to me emotionally and physically, it amuses bystanders. This allows me to interpret any smiles or chuckles as a reaction to my statement and not a comment on my faux pas or as them making fun of me. Additionally, I have rationalized that my subconscious will now be challenged to discover what my first choice would have been in that situation and allow me to perform accordingly next time the situation arises. Since I haven't dropped another unset bowl of Jell-O®, I'd say it's working for me.

On several occasions I have used this calming cue to calm others. In one instance I saw a woman burst into tears as the bottom of her grocery bag ripped out, sending items rolling everywhere. I said, "I'll bet that wasn't your first choice" and started picking up her groceries. The lady, who initially responded, "It certainly wasn't" ultimately ended up chuckling as we collected her groceries together.

Discover phrases to replace those judgmental comments you may be playing in your subconscious. You will find that these calming cues will not only improve your self image, but also make your world a friendlier place.

---

1   Jell-O® is a registered trademark of Kraft Foods Holdings, Inc.

Being appreciative creates a win-win situation.

CLUE #12

THE MAGIC WORDS
ARE STILL MAGIC

Remember when you were a kid and you wanted something? Your mom would say, "What's the magic word?" And you'd say, "Please." She'd give it to you and then say, "What do you say?" And you would respond, "Thank you." Then if you hit your sister, your mother would say, "We don't hit people. What do you say to your sister?" And you'd say, "I'm sorry." At an early age you learned the importance of these words. That hasn't changed. They are just as necessary today. Pretend Mom is watching.

Common courtesies aren't just for company. They belong in every home and in every relationship. They make life so much more pleasant. They are a universal indicator that you respect the contributions the other person is making to your life. Please and thank you should be spoken frequently in your marriage. And when an apology is called for, "I'm sorry" should be spoken without delay.

Every one of us craves to be appreciated. We all long to know that we are making a difference in the lives of the people around us, especially our spouse's. You can make your partner feel appreciated by thanking her when she does anything, big or small, that makes your life easier, better, more beautiful or enjoyable. It's amazing how different "thank you" feels when there is strong eye contact and genuine emotion behind the words.

Being appreciative is not natural for many of us. What was natural for me was to listen to hear if Mike thanked me when I'd gone out of my way to do something nice for him. It was also natural for me to feel a bit martyred if he didn't seem to notice, or if his thanks didn't seem equal to the effort I'd expended on his behalf.

If you don't feel like being pleasant, courteous and kind, act that way and the feelings will come.

Source Unknown

It took us quite a few years of consciously verbalizing our thanks to make the sincerity that belongs with a "thank you" second nature. Now, after just twenty four years of practice, Mike and I are really good at thanking each other sincerely for the little things the other does that make our lives more pleasant.

It feels wonderful to have your efforts acknowledged out loud, and it is unquestionably worth the effort to be sincerely appreciative of each other.

Not sure where the dividing line is between everyday actions and those that should be acknowledged and openly appreciated? Don't hesitate to give your partner the gratitude you would accord a total stranger. If someone mowed your grass and wouldn't accept payment for his service, you would thank him profusely. Yet, we often take for granted these same tasks performed by our partner.

When you ask your partner to do something, always preface your request with "please," even if you are reminding him of something he already agreed to do. The fact that your partner is supposed to do something doesn't take away from the fact that he does it. In fact, the task is probably less agreeable because it is an obligation. Look at your life. Any routine can be boring and unrewarding. A "thank you" upon completion of any task goes a long way in making the job done feel more worthwhile.

Have you ever found yourself smiling as you helped a friend do a chore that you hate to do at home? The task didn't change, your attitude did! Chances are your friend didn't expect your help and voiced his appreciation for your efforts. Making a special effort not to take each other's chores for granted makes them more enjoyable to do or, at least, more bearable.

Being in love is a wonderful feeling, but being loved and appreciated in return can be the most wonderful experience that can happen in your life.

Source Unknown

Being appreciative helps keep any relationship on a more even keel. It involves taking a few minutes each day to remind yourself of the many small sacrifices your partner makes for you and letting her know you appreciate them. Your partner wants to make you happy. You want your partner to be happy. Work at verbalizing your thanks and don't keep score. Being appreciative may not seem to balance out in your relationship right now, this month or even this year.

If you choose to look at each good deed done for you as a small gift to you, it will strengthen your relationship and propel it forward. If you choose to view things done for you as the repayment of a debt, you will most assuredly be miserable.

If you were arrested for kindness,
would there be enough evidence to convict you?

Source Unknown

If being appreciative is not natural for you, don't despair. Taking someone's actions for granted is as much a habit as being appreciative. You can learn to be appreciative, if you are motivated.

Every day, single out one thing that your partner does that you're glad you don't have to do. It doesn't have to be a big deal, anything will do: getting up early, doing dishes, writing checks, walking the dog in bad weather, doing laundry, fixing the car, grocery shopping. Thank your partner for making this contribution to your lives. Although variety is nice, don't worry about finding something different every day; some thanks bear repeating. I probably thank Mike twice a week for going to work every day so that I don't have to.

Thanking your partner just for being who he is will put a smile on his face and a song in his heart. Take time to mention those things that attracted you to your partner: that delightful sense of humor, any compelling physical attributes, mechanical prowess, beautiful manners, artistic abilities or craftsmanship. We all love to be reminded of how special we are.

There is more hunger for love and appreciation in this world than for bread.

Mother Teresa

If you care deeply for each other and have made being appreciative a habit, spats won't last long and they won't leave scars. You will find it difficult to stay mad because you're so used to being supportive and appreciative that you'll want to do and say kind things to each other. When you say or do something you wish you could take back, a sincere, "I'm sorry" will go a long way in opening the door to forgiveness. And after someone apologizes to you, resist the temptation to lecture him. Forgive, then forget.

If you make simple courtesies a habit, it will draw you closer together and help pave the way for emotional intimacy.

---

*A successful marriage is not finding the right person,
but it is being the right person.*

Source Unknown

CLUE # 13

BEND THE
GOLDEN RULE

The Golden Rule is horrible advice for anyone who wants to be happily married. When you do unto others as you would have them do unto you, neither of you gets the results you want. Your spouse wants what he wants, not what you want. You want your efforts to be appreciated, and your spouse isn't going to thank you for doing things your way instead of his. In fact, if you follow the Golden Rule literally and do for your spouse what you would like your spouse to do for you, you may end up being berated for your thoughtlessness.

The bottom line in marriage is seeing a situation through the eyes of your spouse, and then doing for her what she would like done in that situation. Here's where most couples get into trouble. Fortunately, many situations are predictable and you can agree in advance what each of you will do when these arise. Some of the situations you can plan for include:

- When gift giving/receiving for special occasions is expected

109

- Types of gifts you like to receive
- Things you can do to show me you're sorry
- How to approach and where to discuss difficult topics
- Appropriate responses to emotional outbursts
- Identifying what you consider romantic

What constitutes romantic gestures varies greatly from one person to the next. What feels romantic to you? Do you like to receive flowers? Chocolates? Jewelry? Power tools? Mike gets brownie points for bringing me chocolates, power tools or jewelry, but he doesn't bring me flowers. I love flowers, but cut flowers make me sad when they wither and die. And I don't want plants either, because I have a black thumb and it really upsets me when my earnest efforts kill even the heartiest varieties.

One of the most romantic things Mike can do is wash the dishes and clean up the kitchen. These are normally my responsibility and it's a real treat when I don't have to do them. Another one is bringing home a new book from a favorite author, and then encouraging me to drop everything and read it cover to cover. I LOVE it when he does that.

The greatest virtues are those
which are most useful to other persons.

Aristotle

There are so many ways your partner can please you. Letting your spouse know the ins and outs of what will make you happy will make it much more likely she'll be able to do it. For instance, what brings you comfort when you're sick? Some people want to be ignored. Others want to be treated the nurturing way their mother treated them when they were little.

If there is something your partner can do for you to get you through a difficult time, let her know BEFORE a difficult time arises so she can respond appropriately. Here's an example. When Mike would get sick as a little boy, his mom would bring him toast and cambric tea (a blend of boiling water, milk and sugar). Today, if Mike is feeling unwell, an offer of cambric tea and toast never ceases to bring a smile to his face. Notice, I say an offer of cambric tea and toast. While Mike does take me up on my offer to make this every now and then, most of the time, the memory is more appealing than the reality of it.

When I am sick or sad, Mike offers me my childhood comfort foods, raspberry sherbet and 7UP®[1]. I feel coddled and loved when Mike comes home with raspberry sherbet and Diet 7UP® no matter what the occasion.

Direct communications has worked very well for us. We try to keep things simple. When you tell your partner what you want, he can then do it for you. So we talk about virtually everything.

Not everyone chooses this path. It doesn't matter what you choose to do as long as you are both on the same wave length and are both successfully making the other person happy, which is, after all, the bottom line intention of the Golden Rule.

A good example of extremes that work for different couples can be seen in holiday gift giving. At one extreme are Mike and I. We

---

1   7UP® is a registered trademark of Cadbury Schweppes

have not exchanged gifts at any holiday or other special day since we've been married.

When we dated, we both found gift-buying for special days stressful. Mike would buy me beautiful outfits and even though they were the same size as other clothes in my closet, they rarely fit me. I'd end up in tears because I wanted to keep the clothes because Mike bought them for me, while Mike more rationally wanted to return them because they didn't fit me properly.

Ultimately, we found that it works better for us to shop together and buy things when we find them without regard to holidays or special occasions. At holiday time, we celebrate with a hand-written note or card along with a special meal; gifts are notably absent.

My Aunt Carol and Uncle Dick had a very straightforward way of giving gifts. They would each make a list of what they wanted for birthday or Christmas and the other would buy it all and wrap it up. So if my aunt wanted a red robe, a watch and a jazz album for Christmas that's exactly what would be under the tree. My uncle could similarly count on getting his drill, special pipe tobacco and French cuff shirt. Neither asked for anything extravagant and they were never disappointed.

At the opposite extreme are our dear friends Mary and Steve. Mary has a menu of expectations for her gifts and she is adamant about not sharing the details with Steve, or anyone else, for that matter. For each occasion, she expects to receive a certain number of large gifts and a certain number of smaller gifts, a certain number of humorous gifts, a certain number of heart warming gifts and a certain number of practical gifts. She gives hints all year long which she expects Steve to pick up on. She is dead serious about expecting him to deliver the goods and he knows it. As the holiday approaches the tension rises. Did he pay attention? Will the gifts pass the test?

Now, I've seen the gifts opened under their tree after a holiday and the total financial value is not excessive. The emotional cost, from my point of view, is way out of line. But who cares what I think? Seriously! This system works for them which is the only thing that ultimately matters. Mary leaves definite clues and Steve picks up on them. He seems justifiably proud that he got the clues right and she is absolutely delighted as he passes the test each year.

This works for them because they are both willing players in this game. If you are doing something that works for you, bravo! Don't listen to outsiders. Who cares what they think? It only matters what you and your spouse think.

Do not do unto others as you would that they should do unto you. Their tastes may not be the same.

George Bernard Shaw

Obviously, being in tune with each other's expectations is key to giving the other person what they are looking for. We all have rituals that make us feel noticed, cared for and loved. Sharing meaningful rituals with your spouse will allow her to respond appropriately. You will identify your expectations as you complete the questionnaire in the Section V.

Suffice it to say here, you should implement the spirit of the Golden Rule rather than a literal interpretation if you want to be happily married.

Every life has its dark and cheerful hours.
Happiness comes from choosing which to remember.

Author Unknown

CLUE # 14

MENTAL KEEPSAKES

W hat kind of mental scrapbook are you compiling for your
marriage? Are you stockpiling positive images or hanging
onto old hurts and disappointments?

If you're harboring negative images and emotions, stop it right
now. You can not possibly be happy in your marriage. Your marriage
is worth your effort to make it happier. The first step is to dump
those old hurts and disappointments you're dragging around.

Generally speaking, the happiness in your marriage will be
reflected by the memories you keep. If you want to be happily married,
focus on the good stuff. Consider holding onto only those memories
that you would want to showcase to your friends and family.

- When your partner does something nice for you, remember
  it forever and let her know you haven't forgotten.
- If your partner does something that disappoints you or hurts
  you, talk about it as soon as you can do so without aggra-
  vating the situation, then put it behind you and never bring
  it up again. Forgive and forget...forever.

Your happiness is your choice. Selectively holding on to only positive memories will improve your overall happiness.

HE SAID:

When asked his secret of love, being married fifty-four years to the same person, he said, "Ruth and I are happily incompatible."

Billy Graham

SHE SAID:

A good marriage is the union of two good forgivers.

Ruth Bell Graham

CLUE # 15

LET YOUR ACTIONS
SAY, "I LOVE YOU"

Have you ever noticed that people think couples are cute when they are dizzy in love while they're dating? Did you ever stop to ask yourself why this same behavior by this same couple is seen as abnormal, irritating or outright stomach-turning once they get married?

It's sad but true. You can tell if a couple is dating or married by the tone of someone's voice when he says:

"She's got him wrapped around her little finger."

"He's got her number."

"He's whipped."

"She is under his spell."

Why do you suppose that is? Why is it okay to openly demonstrate your love while you're dating, but when you marry you're supposed to keep your feelings for your partner to yourself? I think it's most likely to stem from the inability to imagine the complete power and joy of genuine, reciprocated love.

Now, if you're sitting there thinking, "We don't just have genuine, reciprocated love, we have unconditional love," I don't buy that for a minute. Married love is highly conditional. If it were unconditional, divorce would never occur. Couples would forgive each others' weaknesses and transgressions and go on loving each other for life, just as they do delinquent children.

The reality is that married love is predicated on the other person loving you back. I'll love you as long as you love me. This may sound harsh, but this is the way we live our lives. Think about people who have been dumped, jilted or divorced. These individuals are expected to get over it and get on with their lives. People who remain in love with someone who has stopped loving them are considered to be fixated, living in a dream world or not handling things very well.

That doesn't sound all that encouraging, does it? But it's meant to be. It's meant to suggest that you forget about what other people think and openly demonstrate your love for your spouse forever. Why? Because doing what everyone else is doing isn't working! Think about it. If your partner doesn't experience your love on a day to day basis through your actions, your love for your partner may unconsciously start to be questioned.

Actions speak louder than words.

Aesop's Fables

You can't force your partner to act on his love for you, but you can motivate yourself to act on your love for him. Regularly ask yourself, "Do my actions say I love you?"

*Marriage is not just spiritual communion,
it is also remembering to take out the trash.*

Dr. Joyce Brothers

The following example had wide-ranging impact on our relationship. We'd been married about three years when Mike and my mom were discussing getting dinner from a carry-out place. Mike, a meat and potatoes man, knew that Mom and I love Chinese food. He suggested that she pick up Chinese food for the two of us while he would make himself something. Mom didn't want anyone to have to cook so she offered to get Mike his favorite chicken.

At this point, Mike had a revelation. He said, "This is crazy. If I had to cut off my arm to save Charlie's life, I wouldn't hesitate for a minute. Here, I won't even eat Chinese food when I know that would give her so much pleasure. Forget the chicken. It's about time I learned to eat Chinese food."

Much to my surprise and delight, he did!

*The ordinary arts we practice every day at home
are of more importance to the soul
than their simplicity might suggest.*

Sir Thomas More

The domino effect an action like that can have is amazing. Mike has worked to broaden his palate considerably - he even eats vegetables! This makes it more fun for me to cook. It also serves as a daily reminder of his love for me. And when I see him eating something he didn't eat before, it makes me want to do something special for him.

A couple important notes are due here. First, the fact that he started eating a wider range of foods didn't obligate me to make any changes whatsoever. We're not earning points or keeping score. However, while I didn't have to do anything, I was so delighted and excited about this change that I was inspired to look for ways I could show him that I understood how big an effort he was making for me on an ongoing basis.

Secondly, it's important to note that the initiative for the change had to come from Mike. Had I attempted to twist his love for me into a source of guilt or form of threat by saying, "If you really loved me, you'd eat Chinese food," it would have led to harsh words. Believe me, Mike would not be eating Chinese food, broccoli or asparagus today.

---

*Change has a considerable psychological impact
on the human mind.
To the fearful it is threatening
because it means that things may get worse.
To the hopeful it is encouraging
because things may get better.
To the confident it is inspiring
because the challenge exists to make things better.*

King Whitney Jr.
Laura Moncur's Motivational Quotations

CLUE #15: LET YOUR ACTIONS SAY, "I LOVE YOU"

The reality of your relationship is up to you – not your friends, not your family, not even your spouse. You must take responsibility for making your relationship everything you'd hoped it would be. Take that first step. Let your actions tell your partner that you love her.

Oh, yes. When your friends razz you that your wife keeps you on a pretty tight rein, put them in their place. Tell them, "There's no place I'd rather be. She's the best."

Being married is like having somebody permanently in your corner, it feels limitless, not limited.

Gloria Steinem, Feminist
upon marrying for the first time at age 66 in 2000

Talents differ.
Be sincere in your encouragement.

CLUE # 16

CHEERLEADERS MAKE BETTER LOVERS

Going to bed with a cheerleader is a common fantasy. When you're married you both have an opportunity to do this. Now, we don't mean with cute costumes and role playing (although that is okay, too); we mean you should each be a cheerleader for the other.

With cheerleaders, attitude is everything. They're positive, upbeat, supportive, encouraging and enthusiastic. Their spirit propels their team forward.

Find the good -- and praise it.

Alex Haley

THE CLUES
TO MASTERING MARRIAGE

Wouldn't you love to have someone who's always cheering you on and encouraging your every move? Someone who's consistently supportive of you through gains and setbacks, winning seasons and losing ones? Marriage offers you the opportunity to have just that.

We truly don't believe you can perform to the best of your abilities in any aspect of your life if you are not grounded in a supportive, healthy and happy relationship at home. In fact, if you want to improve your performance in other areas, start with strengthening your marriage and watch those other areas improve.

If you're looking for a simple way to make a good marriage stronger, work on your cheerleading skills. A supportive atmosphere improves any relationship. Imagine the boost your marriage will receive if each of you becomes the other's biggest fan. I'm sure you'll discover, as we have, that knowing someone is solidly in your corner makes everything better in your relationship – work, play, even sex.

I have no way of knowing whether or not you married the wrong person, but I do know that many people have a lot of wrong ideas about marriage and what it takes to make that marriage happy and successful.

I'll be the first to admit that it's possible that you did marry the wrong person. However, if you treat the wrong person like the right person, you could well end up having married the right person after all.

On the other hand, if you marry the right person, and treat that person wrong, you certainly will have ended up marrying the wrong person.

CLUE #16: CHEERLEADERS MAKE BETTER LOVERS

*I also know that it is far more important to be the right
kind of person than it is to marry the right person.
In short, whether you married the right or
wrong person is primarily up to you.*

Zig Ziglar

Many people assume that they will get a supportive partner when they marry, but this doesn't always happen. Some people aren't supportive of their mates on all issues, some seem critical of virtually everything their partners do. It doesn't have to be this way for you if you make it a point to be supportive of each other.

We always try to be supportive of each other, however, there are times when we have serious reservations about something the other wants to do. In these cases, we voice our differences of opinion early on before a final decision is made. Once we agree to a course of action, we set aside our dissenting views and support our partner whole-heartedly.

A good example of this is the purchase of our current car, a 2000 Chevy Camaro with T-tops. Mike had wanted to buy this car since the model was first introduced in 1993. I didn't like the car because I found it uncomfortable and it had minimal trunk space. Finally, in 2004, after Mike had lusted after this car for ten years, I told him to go ahead and buy it if he could find one we could afford (remember, we always pay cash). You can temper your agreement any way you want. I promised not to complain about the car for one year.

The year of no complaints ended May 31, 2005. Although I am no longer obligated to hold my tongue, I have continued to do so.

Why? During this past year I have seen how much Mike loves driving this car. My complaining might ruin his pleasure. You might say that sometimes the most supportive thing you can do is "nothing."

We're constantly striving for success, fame and comfort,
when all we really need to be happy
is someone...to be enthusiastic about.

H. Jackson Brown

It's tough to be neutral in marriage. Usually it's fairly cut and dried; you're either on the same side or you're not. If you're not helping your spouse move toward a happy future, you're probably going to be perceived as part of the obstacles she must overcome. This will put you at odds in your marriage. This is not a good thing.

Why not make a concerted effort to switch to cheerleader mode and support each other in everything you do? I'm not talking about one of you giving up your life in selfless support of the other. I'm talking about each of you taking a genuine interest in the other's activities and offering encouragement and support in these endeavors.

- If your wife has a company golf outing, the best encouragement might be making sure she gets the first turn in the bathroom, making the coffee while she showers and offering her your car for the day because it's easier to get her golf bag in and out of your trunk.
- One thing Mike will do for me is polish my shoes. I'll be racing around like a crazy person and suddenly I'll catch a

glimpse of Mike shining my shoes. It really makes me feel loved and supported to have him take care of this detail for me. I always head out the door in a better mood because he's made this thoughtful and supportive gesture.

And don't forget your role as cheerleader after the event as well. Debrief and find out how the day went. If things went well, celebrate together. If things didn't go well, brainstorm what could be done to make the next time better.

- Highest round of golf by 20 strokes? Sign up for golf lessons together or plan to spend a few hours at the driving range and putting green.
- Fishing trip ruined by cold, rainy weather? Plan to pack sweatshirts and ponchos, games, books, drawing tablets and cards for the next trip.

There are always little things that you can do. Ultimately these little things are not so little. They reflect the love you have for your spouse in big ways.

Don't know how to help or encourage? Ask. Be there for each other. Wear your team colors proudly. When you cheer wildly with enthusiasm and abandon, you'll find that cheerleaders not only have more fun, they really do make better lovers.

If something comes to life in others because of you, then you have made an approach to immortality.

Norman Cousins

---

*Teamwork is the fuel that allows common people
to attain uncommon results.*

Source Unknown

MARRIAGE, THE EXTREME TEAM SPORT

We believe marriage is the most demanding team sport ever devised – more demanding than any extreme sport on TV. It is challenging, high risk and demands finesse and timing. There are unexpected twists and turns over an unknown course. And, whether you succeed or fail, marriage is the most expensive game you will ever play in terms of time, money and effort expended.

Not athletic? Not to worry. Marriage is a sport where your physical prowess is much less important than your game plan, attitude and team skills. In fact, having an inflexible attitude is much more of a handicap than any physical limitations you may have.

Never been part of a team before? Not a problem. Sometimes you may actually have an advantage over experienced team players because you will bring a fresh perspective to the game.

Played on teams as long as you can remember? Chances are you'll still have a lot to learn. The marriage team is unlike other teams you've been on, because there is no opposition, only goals to achieve.

If you're going to play, play to win. Here are pitfalls you'll face:

1. There is no rule book and each player discovers the unwritten rules as the game progresses.
2. There are no position descriptions.
3. There is no referee to make sure you play fair or to whom you can signal for a time out.
4. Every day is game day, and you can't win if both members don't fully participate.
5. No training is required, in fact, rookies are starters from day one.
6. Choice of teammates was completely voluntary, a fact that is often forgotten in finger-pointing and blame games.
7. If one member is primarily concerned with personal success, victory is difficult to achieve.

---

*Teamwork is what the Green Bay Packers were all about.
They didn't do it for individual glory.
They did it because they loved one another.*

Vince Lombardi, Green Bay Packers' Coach

---

8. If someone is keeping score, the team can't win.
9. There is no second string and substitutes are not allowed.
10. You often have fewer fans than you need and more coaches than you want.
11. There is no off-season to recuperate and train.
12. There are a limited number of outstanding players to emulate.

---

*The strength of the team is each individual member...
the strength of each member is the team.*

Coach Phil Jackson, Chicago Bulls & LA Lakers

There are 'problems' and there are real problems.
The vast majority of us don't have real problems.
Our failure to appreciate the difference
constitutes a colossal distortion of thinking -
which has served to effectively destroy more lives
than all war and disease combined.

Quoted by Gary W. Fenchuk in *Timeless Wisdom*

WANTS, NEEDS
AND PREFERENCES

We are going to let you in on a terrific secret that may change the way you view the world. It certainly had a tremendous impact on us. Mike happened upon this idea at a garage sale when he picked up a book called *Handbook to Higher Consciousness*[1]. The language in the book is dated, but this concept is timeless!

Here's our recap of the key points:

- The importance that events and objects play in our lives is learned.
- We can choose to change the importance we attach to these things at will.
- Choosing to reduce the importance we give things in our lives will not only reduce the conflict we experience but also increase our happiness.

The key to the secret is recognizing your wants, needs and preferences. The objective is to minimize your wants and needs and

---

1 Keyes, Ken, Jr., *Handbook to Higher Consciousness, Fifth Edition,*
Living Love Publications, St. Mary, Kentucky, 1978

maximize your preferences. Once you get a grasp of this idea, you will have the option of changing the importance of everything in your life. The potential impact on your personal happiness is absolutely amazing.

Most people seek after what they do not possess and are thus enslaved by the very things they want to acquire.

Anwar El-Sadat

NEEDS

Needs are anything necessary to sustain life. We instinctively fight to our death to obtain our needs. Humans have two kinds of needs, physical and emotional. Our physical needs are air, water, food and shelter; we will literally die if our physical needs are not met. Our emotional needs include our intrinsic values and beliefs that define our personality; we figuratively die when our emotional needs are not met.

In this country, most people have very few, if any, unmet physical needs, but many of us have artificially elevated things and situations into the needs category. We reveal things we are treating as needs when we act as if we will die if we don't get them. These needs exist only in our minds.

Some people are so convinced of these perceived needs that they actually die rather than give up their car or wallet to someone who is willing to use force to take them. Some of these people died for their need of the object itself (the car or money) while others died for their need to be right, to have the last word or to be treated with respect.

CLUE #18: WANTS, NEEDS AND PREFERENCES

WANTS

Wants are those things that are necessary to sustain happiness. While you might not be willing to fight to the finish to get one of your wants, you can be very unhappy and stressed out if you do not get whatever it is that you want or feel you deserve.

What difference does it make how much you have? What you do not have amounts to much more.

Seneca

PREFERENCES

Preferences are things that are nice to have or have happen, but you're indifferent or only slightly disappointed if you don't get them or they don't happen. When a preference is not met, there is little impact on your life or your happiness.

We are happy in proportion to the things we can do without.

Henry David Thoreau

You'll notice that both wants and needs are accompanied by escalating degrees of negative emotions when they are not met. To differentiate between things you hold as wants and those you hold as needs, examine how you feel when you don't get something. If you are significantly disappointed or angry when you do not get something, you wanted it. If you were furious or despondent that you didn't get it, you probably felt you needed it. These unmet wants and needs add considerable conflict to our lives and significantly reduce our happiness.

---

*The greater part of our happiness or misery depends
on our dispositions and not on our circumstances.
We carry the seeds of the one or the other
about with us in our minds wherever we go.*

Martha Washington

We develop our wants and needs by mimicking friends and family, as well as through our exposure to advertising, magazines, television and movies, even legislated entitlement programs. Anything that shows us what the average person has or should have adds to our expectation of what *we* should have. Ultimately, expectations can become wants or even needs. After all, we're all above average, aren't we? It logically follows then that we deserve to have more than the average person.

Are wants and needs wrong? Absolutely not. There is nothing inherently wrong with wanting something or feeling you need something ... unless not having it diminishes your happiness.

Here's the best part, when you are able to recognize that you are holding something in your life as a want or a need and then consciously choose to lower its importance to the level of preference, you will no longer be a victim of its power over you. Imagine how much dissatisfaction, stress and unhappiness you can get rid of just like that when you reduce your wants and needs to preferences!

Happiness is not having what you want.
It is wanting what you have.

Unknown

This is good stuff, isn't it?

This tool is amazing. It offers you the opportunity to change the way you look at the world. We have found that this concept has allowed us to be much happier with many situations we encounter. I'm going to give you two real-life examples where a need was changed to a preference so you get a better idea of how you might apply this in your life.

Road Rage

Mike believed that people who drive in the fast lane should drive as fast as traffic allows. If he were behind someone who could be driving faster, he got upset. He wanted THEM to drive faster or move out of HIS lane. Sometimes he'd get so mad that veins would pop out on his forehead and he'd practically spit as he denounced them under his breath. Mike had elevated driving fast in the fast lane to the level of a need.

Was there anything wrong with needing to drive fast in the fast lane (ignore the fact that this might involve speeding)? From Mike's perspective, the biggest thing wrong was that this unmet need was negatively impacting his quality of life.

Once we learned about wants, needs and preferences, Mike made a conscious decision to downgrade his need to have people drive fast in the fast lane to a preference. The change was dramatic. Now he is a much more even-tempered driver. When Mike encounters someone driving slow in the fast lane, he changes lanes and continues on his way. The slow car no longer raises his blood pressure or negatively impacts his day ... although some days I'll still hear him remind himself, "It's only a preference that this idiot drives the speed limit..."

Eating Habits

Our daughter, Christina, and her husband, Brian, moved to Japan for several years because of Brian's job in the Navy. Christina was one of those people who never wanted any of the food on her plate touching any of the other food on her plate. She avoided sauces and runny foods because they would contaminate adjoining foods. She never ate anything she didn't recognize.

When we found out they would be living in a Japanese community, Mike and I thought, "Poor Brian." We fully expected Christina to be a real pill about the food. Imagine my surprise when I visited her and found her eating and enjoying all the native foods.

When I asked her how she had overcome her aversion to mixed and unfamiliar foods, she told me it was pretty easy. She kept reminding herself "It's only a preference that my foods not touch each other. It's only a preference that I know what these things are." And after the first couple of meals, it truly became a preference. The fact that foods were mixed together and unfamiliar no longer mattered to her at all.

It's your life. Don't be a victim of circumstances that are fully within your control. Recognize that you make choices every day that impact your happiness and add conflict to your life. You can choose to change this. Make your wants, needs and preferences work for you.

Just think how happy you would be
if you lost everything you have right now...
and then got it back again.

Author Unknown

Differing expectations can
cause problems to grow.

CLUE # 19

EVERY COUPLE
NEEDS AN
EMOTIONAL PRENUPTIAL™

We've all heard about prenuptial agreements. Sometimes referred to as prenups, the more complete name for them is financial prenuptials. These legal documents spell out how marriage partners have agreed to divide their assets if they divorce. These agreements are drafted prior to marriage and only implemented when the marriage is over.

Isn't that sad? The primary purpose of the most common document used to prepare for marriage defines the dissolution of that marriage. Wow. Here a couple has spent a lot of time, effort, emotion and money to create a document that no one hopes to ever implement.

We want to change that. No, we don't want more people implementing their financial prenups! We want to provide couples with a prenuptial they will want to implement every day, one that will strengthen their marriage and help them grow happier and more in love each year.

TADA! Introducing the Emotional Prenuptial™.

While a financial prenuptial safeguards assets during divorce, an Emotional Prenuptial™ safeguards happiness during marriage. Doesn't that make a lot more sense? If you have physical assets you want to protect, you'll still need a legally binding financial prenuptial drafted by a licensed attorney. But if you create an Emotional Prenuptial™ as well, and use it every day, you'll have a much better chance of never needing to implement your financial prenup. We love this.

---

*You did the best that you knew how.
Now that you know better, you'll do better.*

Maya Angelou

Remember back in the "By Way of Introduction" section I told you how a chance meeting with Ken Burley transformed Mike's and my chances for success in marriage? Ken told us to **separately** write out our expectations of marriage, compare these expectations and then agree **in writing** how we would resolve any differences we discovered. When we were done, we had laid the foundation for an incredible marriage that has not only weathered some really tough times; it has allowed us to sail through them unscathed, emerging more in love than ever.

In essence, we created an Emotional Prenuptial™. We refer to it as our Marriage Pact™. It spells out the individual rights and responsibilities that we've agreed to live by in our marriage.

Creating your Marriage Pact™ together is the most wonderful gift you can give your partner and your relationship. As you create your ground rules, you will outline what you want from marriage. Identifying what you want is the first step to getting it.

Consciously creating your Marriage Pact™ is the only way you can be assured that you are operating on the same wave length and have the same expectations for your relationship and of each other.

---

*We live in an era of revolution-
the revolution of rising expectations.*

Adlai Stevenson

You probably didn't know that every marriage has a Marriage Pact™. Study any couple and you'll see their pact in action:
- How do they spend money?
- How much do they save?
- Do they always buy the best?
- Do they cook at home or eat out?
- Who takes out the garbage, does the laundry, walks the dog, sorts the mail, pays the bills?
- How do they reach decisions?
- How are disagreements handled?
- Who defers to whom?

Where do these rules come from? They come from the experience of the partners, their observations of other relationships and their preconceived notions and best guesses of what makes a good

145

marriage. Most Marriage Pacts™ develop haphazardly, generally by the trial and error merging of unspoken expectations. Consequently, few couples know the rules of their relationship. This is a shame.

Think about it. How can you live up to rules when you don't know that they are? Or when you find you don't share the same ones?

Is it any surprise there are so many unhappy marriages? Working together to lay the ground rules for your marriage is one of the fastest ways to get to really know your partner. In fact, once your Marriage Pact™ is complete, you'll know each other better than many couples who have been married 25 years or more.

---

*You've picked the right person,
now pick the right path that
will enrich your future together.*

Mike & Charlie

We think you'll discover, as we did, that you'll like your spouse even better now that you truly know him. Creating our Marriage Pact™ unquestionably deepened our love and sense of commitment to each other. It also dramatically increased our level of emotional intimacy and permanently increased the passion in our relationship.

It is easiest to create a pact before you are married, before you create barriers between yourselves and before an argument reveals you've broken a rule you didn't know existed. If you're not yet married, terrific! Create your pact now and get your marriage off to its best possible start. If you are already married you have a greater challenge, but a greater motivation. You have probably already discovered where some of your expectations differ from your partner's.

The rest of your lives together will hopefully be a very long time. Formalizing your Marriage Pact™ can help you smooth over trouble spots you may already be experiencing. It can also help minimize differences that haven't yet become problems. Your Marriage Pact™ will make your relationship even more enjoyable.

Grow old along with me.
The best is yet to be.

Robert Browning

CAUTION:

**A Marriage Pact™ is a VOLUNTARY guide,
NOT A LEGAL DOCUMENT.
If you have assets you want to protect or agreements
you want to make legally binding,
SEEK LEGAL ASSISTANCE.
IF IN DOUBT, CONSULT A LAWYER.**

You might think you don't need to create a Marriage Pact™, but you'd be wrong. Every couple will greatly benefit by formalizing their Marriage Pact™, because it will help you:

- really get to know each other
- know that you are on the same page on important issues
- make it easier to please each other
- minimize conflict
- understand what is expected of you
- know what you can expect from your partner
- develop a team mentality
- develop unshakeable confidence in each other
- feel solidly grounded in your marriage
- cultivate emotional intimacy
- experience more passion
- grow your love exponentially
- create a safe haven for each of you
- become more confident in every aspect of your life
- make you happier than you thought possible

The best part is that it is truly fun and extremely rewarding. This is an unparalleled opportunity to make the rest of your life together everything you hoped it could be.

Creating an Emotional Prenuptial™ is the most important concept in the book. Creating our Marriage Pact™ was the single best investment of time and effort that we made in our marriage. This is so important that Part III of this book is totally dedicated to guiding you through the process of creating a Marriage Pact™ that meets the unique needs of your relationship.

The future is not a result of choices among alternative paths offered by the present, but a place that is created -- created first in the mind and will, created next in activity. The future is not some place we are going to, but one we are creating. The paths are not to be found, but made, and the activity of making them, changes both the maker and the destination.

John Schaar, Professor Emeritus of Political Philosophy
University of California at Santa Cruz

---

*Choosing a love, and then, being strong enough to live up
to your commitment of love, is the essence of love.*

Source Unknown

CLUE # 20

DON'T LET YOUR
WARRANTY EXPIRE

Did you ever buy anything that was guaranteed, but when a problem arose you found the guarantee wasn't worth the paper it was written on? Many people are similarly undependable. As soon as their commitments aren't convenient, they do what they please, ignore their promises and the responsibilities they agreed to assume. Don't do this to each other.

Neither of you can eliminate this problem alone. Even if one of you is willing to give 200%, it won't make up for an uncommitted partner. It takes two committed individuals to safeguard a marriage.

Trust is central to the success of any relationship and fundamental in every marriage.

- Do you trust your partner?
- Do you believe he intends to live up to his commitments?
- Can your partner trust you to keep your word?

When you marry, you pledge your love till death do you part.

151

---

*Motto for the bride and groom:
We are a work in progress with a lifetime contract.*

Phyllis Koss

Your agreements should carry this same lifetime guarantee. Make only those promises you are willing to live with. Create only those agreements you believe are fair to both of you - agreements each of you feels you will be able to honor forever.

Many people will discuss issues, make agreements, even put them in writing, but when they aren't convenient, they'll ignore them. Don't fall into this trap! It will undermine your relationship. Plan to live with your agreements even when it seems almost impossible. When Mike and I got married, we made a number of agreements that were not easy to live by. We lived by them anyway. It has drawn us closer and fostered mutual admiration and respect.

You can do this too.

The success of your relationship ultimately boils down to your integrity. Can your partner count on you to keep your word? Your relationship is important to you. Keep your word.

Unshared expectations can be highly disruptive.

PART III

HOW TO CREATE YOUR EMOTIONAL PRENUPTIAL™

Just be yourself.
A good exercise is to sit down
and go through all the major areas of your life
and decide how each would be different
if the only person you had to impress was you.

Simplify Your Life, daily calendar

TO THINE OWN SELF
BE TRUE

Before you can decide on the rules you will live by in your marriage, it is critical to identify your personal marital expectations. If this sounds like an overwhelming task, don't worry. We've included a questionnaire in Part V of this book that will help you formulate your ideas and will assist you through the process of discovering exactly what it is that each of you want out of your marriage.

As you answer each question, you will be identifying assumptions you hold about being married, married life, your life goals, your role as a spouse, and the role of your spouse. You'll also be defining your expectations of your marriage. Questions are grouped by topic and topics are listed alphabetically.

We can't stress this enough:
DO THIS ALONE...as in WITHOUT YOUR PARTNER.
AND DO IT IN WRITING.

Don't consult each other or hint what your responses are. Don't compare notes. It will work best if you are physically separated whenever you work on your responses.

Answer the questions the way you would like things to be if you ruled your world, because you do! At this point, don't worry about what your partner wants. Trust that he'll tell you. Your job is to tell your partner what you want.

We can't over-emphasize how important it is for you to explore *your* feelings. Don't try to second-guess what your partner wants you to say. She wants you to be yourself. What is important to *you*? How do *you* feel? What are *you* looking for? What are *your* preferences? *Your* wants? What will make *you* happy?

You can live a lifetime and, at the end of it, know more about other people than you know about yourself.

Beryl Markham, *West with the Night*

This is not an exercise about changing yourself. You're not looking to create a Stepford marriage where partners have subordinated all personal interests for the good of the relationship or the benefit of their partners. Your goal is not subservience or submissiveness.

What you are striving for is a clear statement of who each of you are, so your marriage can reflect your personalities and allow you to thrive both individually and as a couple. Don't undermine your efforts by trying to be anyone but yourself.

ANSWER ALL THE QUESTIONS

As you complete the questionnaire, don't pass anything over. An item that seems unimportant to you today may be very important to your partner or this item could become important to you later should your circumstances unexpectedly change. Try to envision the future. Avoid problems. Assume that each item is important to your partner and address it with the respect you would like to be accorded.

- If you feel you've previously reached agreement on a subject, write down your understanding of it anyway.
- If you think of something that isn't included in the book, make note of the topic, your assumptions about the topic and discuss it with your partner.
- If you are writing in a notebook, it will be helpful if answers are complete so it is easy to tell what question you are answering. For example, for the question: Do you smoke? It will be easier now to write the word "yes" or "no," but you will have many yes and no answers. It will be much easier when compiling your Marriage Pact™ to see more complete answers, so write, "yes, I smoke" or "no, I don't smoke."
- If and ONLY if a category is completely irrelevant both now and in your future together, may you skip it. For example, if you are married, you may skip the "wedding" section, but do NOT skip the Adult Children section, even if you have no children at this time.

BE HONEST

A major advantage of creating our Marriage Pact™ is knowing that each of us is accepted and wanted just the way we are. It has freed us to love and be loved more completely. This knowledge of acceptance has been key to achieving intimacy in our relationship. This will be true for you, as well.

The questionnaire is included in Part V of this book. Each of you will write your answers in a separate notebook. If you prefer a write-in notebook that includes the questions or would like to complete your questionnaire on-line, information on these options is shown on page 252.

If you are both straightforward and honest in answering your questionnaires, you will have identified your assumptions about marriage and will have given each other a tremendous gift - the key to making each other happy.

The supreme happiness of life
is the conviction of being loved for yourself,
or, more correctly, of being loved in spite of yourself.

Victor Hugo

ENJOY THE PROCESS

This is not a test. There are no right or wrong answers. Take your time. Be honest. Have fun. This is an exciting and empowering undertaking.

Oh, and one last thing. If you think it's going to be time-consuming to answer these questions, you're right. It will be. This portion may take several days or even a few weeks for you to complete. Please take the time to answer the questions and be thorough. This is your best chance to be heard. What you do here will set the stage for your future together.

The changes we need to make to our lives are the obvious ones. But we're often too busy to stop and think about what we need to do to bring them about.
We've been so caught up in the stress and the pressures and the demands of our days that we've gotten out of the habit of thinking about our lives.

Source Unknown

Be sure you fully explore
each other's assumptions.

STEP 2

I LIKE YOU EVEN BETTER
NOW THAT I KNOW YOU

When each of you has answered all the questions in the questionnaire, you are ready to begin the most fun and exciting part of this process: learning about your partner. This is an incredible adventure.

Over the period of a few days, you will learn more about each other than many couples learn throughout their entire lives together. Think of the tremendous advantage you will have. You will know how to make each other happy and what is expected of you. What a boon to your relationship!

You will get to know each other by systematically comparing your answers to the questions and discussing any additional comments or assumptions you noted. In this process, you will discover your similarities and differences. In the next step, Union Contract Negotiations, we'll suggest various ways you can address these differences.

The first step is to identify a time and place for your discussions. It is critical that you not be interrupted or distracted during this time

- no family, no friends, no children, no phones, no pets. Ideally, you will have a room with nothing in it but the two of you, a place for each of you to sit where you can easily see each other and a writing surface. Be sure you dress comfortably so you can relax and get down to the task. While some couples have done this at home, to be sure we'd be alone, we rented a cabin with no phone, radio or TV for a three day weekend.

Set aside time to compare your answers. Discussions generated may be lengthy. It may take several days to cover all topics. We took about 20 hours over the three days for this process. One couple wrote that they timed their discussions; it took them 40 hours to discuss everything. No matter how long it takes, it will be time well spent.

You need to be able to sit down together and talk things through until you reach agreement on each issue that comes up.

This type of open discussion was new territory for both Mike and me. I was used to bursting into tears to get my way and Mike tended to get sarcastic and caustic when things weren't going as he wanted. Since neither of these reactions is conducive to a productive conversation, we agreed to some ground rules for our discussions.

While the ground rules didn't totally eliminate our unproductive behavior, they did give us a framework within which to operate. Occasionally, we had to call a time out to get our emotions under control, but as we experienced success in coming to our first agreement, and then another and another, things got easier.

You may find it helpful to put ground rules into effect as you share your answers and create your pact. Here are the ground rules we followed. We signed them and posted the list nearby as a reminder of our intentions. You may want to use our rules as they are, or feel free to modify them to meet your needs.

GROUND RULES FOR
OUR MARRIAGE PACT˝ DISCUSSIONS

We believe that by addressing our differences now, before they become problems: each of us will know what is expected of us in our marriage; and we can permanently eliminate most discord from our relationship. This benefit is worth any pain or discomfort we incur while addressing these differences head-on now. With this in mind, I promise to:

1. Be as nice as I possibly can be (e.g., no name calling or bullying).
2. Retain my sense of humor.
3. Remember that you love me and want both of us to be happy.
4. Stay focused on the task at hand (e.g., no phone calls, newspapers, TV or radio and no distracting each other with kissing, etc.).
5. Leave the room ONLY at pre-arranged breaks (e.g., If I find that I have stormed out of the room despite my best intentions, I will turn right around and walk back in).
6. Be honest about my wants and needs and not try to guess what I'm expected to say.
7. View everything said in the best possible light (e.g., when something said appears hurtful or cruel, I will presume things came out wrong, look for the kernel of truth and not take offense).
8. Maintain a positive attitude (e.g., no ranting, raving or carrying on unproductively).
9. Accept emotions that arise, pull myself back together and get back on task (e.g., it's okay to get angry or cry, but let's not dwell on this).
10. Reach our objective (e.g., I will not allow unrelated activities and conversations to distract us from laying the groundwork for a fabulous future together).

Signed:_____and_____

Begin to compare answers. You may want to start at the beginning and go through the topics in sequence. If one topic is dominating your thoughts, you may want to begin with it to get it out of the way. Or you may prefer to start with topics that you don't feel strongly about or you expect you're in agreement on so you can ease into the process.

Take turns being the first to share your answers. One of you reads the first question out loud along with his answer, then the partner reads her answer to that question. If your answers match, breathe a huge sigh of relief (just kidding) and move on to the next question. Change who goes first for the next question.

The first duty of love is to listen.

Paul Tillich

When you are in agreement on a question, write down your mutual understanding on a piece of paper. This list of agreements will become your Marriage Pact¨. You're going to have quite a few agreements, so it will be helpful to use a notebook to keep them together.

If your answers differ, you will need to decide how you will handle your differences. The information in the following chapter will help you do this.

A great marriage is not when the 'perfect' couple comes together. It is when an imperfect couple learns to enjoy their differences.

Dave Meurer, *Daze of Our Wives*

Either you both win or you both lose.
For every argument that has a victor,
a little piece of your marriage dies.

UNION CONTRACT NEGOTIATIONS

We believe that any two people who love and respect each other and are willing to assume responsibility for the success of their marriage can create an enduring, happy marriage. Your success will hinge on your honesty in addressing your differences, your good faith in negotiating terms you are willing to live with and your integrity in abiding by your agreements throughout your marriage.

As you come across differences in your questionnaire answers, consider how strongly you are attached to your answer. Is it a want, a need or a preference to you? If something is a preference to you and your partner feels strongly about the topic, then it would make sense that you would agree to your partner's position in this area.

If something feels like it is part of who you are, then it is one of your needs and should be protected accordingly. Things like religion, having children, doing drugs and other belief and value-related topics are apt to be needs. In some of these areas you may feel comfortable agreeing to live and let live. For example, you may acknowledge your differing religious beliefs and agree that you will each practice your separate faiths without interference from the other. If you choose this path, be certain to discuss how you will handle this area should you have children. Then be prepared to live by these agreements and defend whatever position you choose to your families.

If something is a want, can you downgrade it to a preference? If this became the deal breaker in your relationship, would you still hold on to this want? Mike and I frequently look at things through this deal breaker filter. Is this issue more important than our relationship? This was especially helpful to us as we worked to maintain, or regain, our perspective as we developed our Marriage Pact™.

While you want to reach agreement, be careful not to burden your relationship with compromises you know you can't live with. It's important that you feel good about the decisions you reach, that you both maintain a caring attitude and that you feel each of you will be able to keep your side of the bargain forever – or until the position is renegotiated in a later review of your Pact. Don't count on an agreement changing, ever.

A marriage is not a competition. There is no such thing as a winner and a loser. Either you both win or you both lose. For every argument that has a victor, a little piece of your marriage dies. Once you have decided how strongly you feel about an issue, you need to work to address that issue until you both feel like winners - or at least until neither one of you feels like a loser.

Quite often the difficult part of a negotiation is identifying the real issue. Don't assume you know what your partner is thinking. Always ask "Why?" And ask this with the intention of learning the answer, not intimidating him into agreeing with you or making him feel like an idiot for his opinion. Talk about the issue until you're sure you understand each other's position.

If, for example, you want to live in a condominium while your partner wants to live in a house, it may not be a problem. Why do each of you feel the way you do?

- It may be that you hate yard work, but would live in a house if your partner were willing to do all the yard work and outside maintenance.
- Maybe your parents never did anything fun because they were always having to work around the house. In this case you might agree to put off a home purchase until you could afford to pay someone to do home maintenance tasks, or you might rent a home from an owner responsible for maintenance.
- If your partner's primary interest in a house is to have a garden, you might live in a condo and participate in a garden co-op.
- If your spouse's primary interest in a house is to build equity and condos don't appreciate as well as houses in your area, perhaps living in an apartment and investing in a triple-net commercial property would offer similar benefits without the inherent responsibility of a house.

There is no right or wrong solution, but some solutions will work better for you. Your task is to propose alternate solutions until you hit on something you both think is reasonable and fair.

DON'T IGNORE ANY AREAS.

---

*The goal in marriage is not to think alike,
but to think together.*

Robert C. Dodds

Care enough to keep talking until you reach an understanding of each other's position. Negotiate until you reach an agreement. It is important that you agree on an issue, agree on a compromised version or agree how you will handle your disagreement. Whatever your final agreement, you will be adding it to your Marriage Pact™ and your partner will expect you to live by it. Resolve these issues today and you'll be able to put them behind you.

Putting something behind you doesn't necessarily mean you'll never run into the issue again, but it does mean you know exactly how this mini drama will play out in your lives. For example, friends of ours disagreed about pets. The husband wanted a large hunting dog and the wife didn't want anything to do with a dog. They compromised with the following agreement:

"Bob may have any one pet of his choosing. Only a housebroken animal will be brought into the house. No pet will ever sleep on our bed. Bob will be solely responsible for his pet. If the pet creates additional housecleaning, Bob agrees to do these cleaning tasks even though he is not usually responsible for housecleaning. Anything the pet breaks gets replaced at Bob's expense from his monthly "fun" money. If Bob is gone overnight, Bob will take the pet with him or find temporary housing for it."

An agreement of this nature takes considerable integrity to uphold, as was the case for Bob and Ellen. In theory, the dog, who was beautifully trained in Bob's presence, was only allowed in the house when Bob was home. Unfortunately, the dog would occasionally sneak inside past an unsuspecting delivery person or guest and wreak havoc when Bob was not there. Ellen would eventually get the dog outside, but there was often considerable damage done. She left the mess created by the dog for Bob. Bob promptly cleaned up when he got home and repaired or replaced anything broken. Period.

Avoiding a topic may create a problem
where none existed.

No blame was ever assigned. No angry words exchanged. And both of them enjoyed telling an occasional story about the dog's exploits. If you make a similar agreement, I hope you will maintain a similar level of integrity in upholding it.

Sometimes you have strong opinions but don't know why. You want something, period. Set the topic aside and come back to it every so often, perhaps every time you finish with another topic.

Think about the problem issue. Don't work at justifying why you are right to feel the way you do. Think back through your experiences with whatever is at issue and try to determine what makes you feel the way you do. There is a reason; eventually, it will become apparent to you. When it does, the depth of your emotion may surprise you. Share your feelings.

I think a man and a woman should choose each other for life, for the simple reason that a long life with all its accidents is barely enough time for a man and a woman to understand each other and...To understand is to love.

William Butler Yeats

Once the real issues have been bared, you can begin searching for ways to fulfill the underlying needs in a mutually satisfactory way.

Sometimes it comes down to who cares more about the subject at hand. If it's still a toss-up, set the issue aside and leave it until the end. You may find that you have several issues on which you're undecided.

If this is the case, look for off-setting issues. You may conclude that he gets to pick where you live and you get to pick whether you live in a condo or a house. Although your friends may feel these categories are not equal, who cares? What matters is that the two of you are satisfied that your agreements will work for both of you.

You may have heard the saying, "A good marriage is like a casserole; only those responsible for it really know what goes in it." No one outside of the two of you will ever understand what is involved in making your marriage work and no one else needs to know any of the compromises and trade-offs you make to ensure the success of your marriage.

How you handle the momentary regrets that inevitably accompany a major decision will greatly impact your happiness. Let's say you've agreed to relocate to take advantage of a unique job opportunity for yourself or your partner. Even though you may be excited about the prospects awaiting you and happy overall that you're moving, you will undoubtedly be homesick from time to time for family, friends or something familiar...even rotten weather!

It has worked for us to be open about our regrets and for the other person to be supportive. Rather than brooding or feeling guilty, we talk about our feelings and do our best to comfort each other. Mike is especially good at bringing me back into balance by getting me laughing and reminiscing about the less than desirable aspects of the path not taken. By being open with each other, these momentary regrets draw us closer.

If you have significantly different views on issues that are very important to each of you, your task will be much harder. While we don't say it's impossible to successfully negotiate tremendous differences, you will both need absolute integrity and it will be critical that you trust each other implicitly.

Ultimately it comes down to which is more important, this issue or your relationship?

Ken Burley (who originally suggested to us that we write down our assumptions about marriage) and his wife Mary faced a crisis of extreme proportions when they were exploring getting married. Ken was an atheist and Mary a passionate Christian. They agreed that they would respect their religious differences and not attempt to convert each other to their respective points of view...but what to do about raising children? Ultimately they agreed not to have children because they didn't feel they could reach an agreement on how to raise their children from a religious standpoint. They felt that their religious differences would make their home a battleground if children became part of the equation, and they didn't want this for themselves or their children. This was a huge decision for a young couple.

They never had children. Ken said there was more than one moment of regret about this decision over the years and that they had explored how they could handle this situation numerous times. Each time they came back to the same conclusion: having children would lead to their divorce and they only wanted to have children if they would raise them together.

Ken and Mary's problem was painful to address. I'm sure there was a huge temptation to skip over this and hope that it would resolve itself in time. PLEASE, PLEASE, PLEASE, PLEASE, PLEASE do not proceed without resolving these issues. Do NOT count on your partner changing her mind to your point of view. The likelihood of this happening is just as slim as the likelihood that you will suddenly change to embrace your partner's point of view.

I know a woman who was so certain she didn't want children that she had her tubes tied in her early twenties. She married a man who knew this and was supposedly okay with not having children.

Almost immediately after their marriage, he began encouraging her to have a reversal of her tubal ligation so they could have children. She doesn't want children, period. He now says that he does. Only time will tell if their marriage lasts, but my bet is that the only thing his prodding nets is a great deal of resentment from his wife.

Problems which are ignored don't go away. They burrow in and fester and rear their heads sooner or later. Eventually, you will have to deal with them. If you wait until the problems crop up in your marriage, they will be accompanied by a tremendous amount of tension and may result in divorce or bitter coexistence.

We believe that two people who love each other can work out most disagreements. However, agreement in some areas, such as having children or doing drugs, is so fundamental to the success of a marriage that if you cannot reach an agreement you are possibly better off not being together. However, before you throw in the towel, please seek counsel from your clergy, a marriage counselor or other trusted professional. She may be able to guide you through to a solution even when you believe your future together is lost.

I often wonder when the wedding couple will realize just how much hard work they've taken on by consecrating that quirky emotion called love into the formal tie of marriage.

Lois Smith Brady, *NY Times* "Vows" columnist

If you plan to share a chore,
a written schedule will avoid confusion.

GET IT IN WRITING

Drafting your Marriage Pact˜ is nothing more than keeping a tally of everything you agreed to during your discussions. When you have discussed all the questions on a topic and agreed how you will address this issue in your relationship, write your agreement(s) on this topic on a new list. This list will be your Marriage Pact˜.

How detailed you make your agreements depends on a number of things:
- how complex or straightforward your agreements are
- whether you are detail or big-picture oriented
- how similar your answers are
- your ability to be succinct
- how betrayed and hurt you felt in a prior relationship

It's important that each of you feel your Marriage Pact˜ reflects everything to which you have agreed. If this takes lengthy verbiage, that is preferable to gaping holes which will undoubtedly lead to misunderstandings later. If one of you wants to go into a great deal more detail than the other, let that person be the scribe and be responsible for getting things clear on paper to your mutual satisfaction.

You are writing the rules for the rest of your life. Take this seriously. Stand up for what is important to you. You are, in large part, determining the quality of your life together. Be sure that what you are doing is consistent with what you want.

---

*I know you thought you understood what I said,
but what you heard isn't what I meant.*

Alan Greenspan

The intent of your Marriage Pact˜ is to create a framework within which you will conduct your relationship. You want to be careful not to create a cage that confines you, a trap certain to sabotage you later, or a goal so lofty you know from the get-go that it is not attainable. For example, you might agree to attend St. Luke's 11:00 service every Sunday.

This might work well for some couples. For others, this could be a cage:

- You can't visit your family for the weekend, attend the Super Bowl, go camping with the Cub Scouts or participate in a weekend walkathon because you have to be at St. Luke's at 11:00 Sunday.

a trap:

- You can't accept a job offer because it is too far away to allow you to attend Sunday services at St. Luke's.

or an impossible goal:

- A long-haul truck driver with a 10 day route will not be in town every Sunday.

Make your agreements as broad as possible while still meeting your objectives. Consider the broader application of the following alternative agreements:

- We will attend a religious service each week and will attend together if at all possible.
- We will attend St. Luke's 11:00 service when we are in town and attend local services when we are on the road.
- We will support the St. Luke community with weekly financial donations, monthly volunteer service and attendance at Sunday services when possible.

Granted, these are not making the same commitment, but for many couples they would be more realistic to follow. Creating something you will follow is the objective here, not establishing a list of New Year's resolutions which will be broken before the year is out.

Remember, it isn't important that you are in agreement on everything. What is important is that you discover now, in a relaxed atmosphere, where you don't agree and how you will cope with these differences.

For example, I assumed that I would not iron. Mike assumed that I would. Our pact states that I would not do any ironing and that Mike would get rid of any clothes that needed ironing, send clothes out to be ironed or plan to iron them himself. Not exactly a compromise, but it worked for us!

Inherent in this agreement is Mike's promise not to whine, try to make me feel guilty or nag me about ironing because we agreed that I won't iron. Had the agreement been that I would iron, it would have been my responsibility to do it without complaining. Mike would have had every right to expect the ironing to be done well and in a reasonable time frame.

Some of your discussion will be strictly informational and may not warrant an official agreement. You don't really need to agree that your partner's favorite color is turquoise, his eyes are blue and his sign is Taurus. You may, however, want to highlight this information on your personal work sheets and keep it with your Marriage Pact‴ for reference.

Only the two of you can decide which topics are informational. If one of you feels strongly about a topic, it belongs in your Marriage Pact‴. I wanted a statement in our agreements that I would not be expected to iron, because I am practically militant about this issue and didn't want there to be any misunderstandings later. You may not feel that strongly about a similar topic, but that's for you to decide. When you come to a topic that is important to you for any reason, spend extra time on it and alert your partner to its significance.

A special topic for us was the Emotions category. Mike's son nicknamed him "Mellow Mike" because of his hot temper. Mike told me that if I could totally ignore his outbursts for ten seconds, it would be out of his system and he would no longer care about whatever set him off. Although it has not always been easy, when I follow his advice I am not drawn into his outbursts and they do not escalate into irrational arguments.

It is easy when you are thin, healthy and full of good intentions to ask your spouse to nag you should you start slipping into bad habits like weight gain, lack of exercise or rising cholesterol levels. Carefully think through any police authority you give your spouse in your agreements. These are bound to be trouble spots later. It can be difficult to have your bad habits pointed out when they start popping up, even though this is what you asked your spouse to do. And, if you expect your partner to react poorly to your agreed-upon-comments, you may avoid saying anything even though you promised to speak up.

Be sure you want your partner to point out your
failings before you give him police power.

Ignoring an agreement may undermine the integrity of your entire Marriage Pact". If you find that you are not implementing one of your agreements, the agreement should be revised. We'll talk about updating your agreements in the next chapter.

Define now what you want your spouse to do when you have a problem. It may be helpful to use family members who have similar problems as bench marks. In our case, Mike's father had a stroke. His recovery was hindered when he didn't follow his doctor's orders on exercise and diet. Should Mike have a stroke and take on his dad's non-compliance, I am to do whatever it takes to coerce Mike into following doctor's orders. This includes any tactic that won't land me in jail!

When you have gone through all the topics and written out all your agreements, your Marriage Pact" is complete. Sign and date your Marriage Pact" and keep it in a safe place. Refer to it as needed for guidance. Don't cut corners. Your Marriage Pact" absolutely **MUST** be in writing. If you would like a formal Marriage Pact" keepsake in which to write your agreements, see page 252.

Your Marriage Pact" is a voluntary guide, not a legal document. If you have issues you want or need to make legally binding, have an attorney draft those documents before you get married or commingle assets.

The palest ink is better than the best memory.

Chinese Proverb

If you want to change an agreement, you must
gain your partner's approval without coercion.

ON-GOING
MARRIAGE MAINTENANCE

After you are married for a while, you will probably see some things differently. A move to a new area, a significant change in income, the birth of a child, a shift in work loads or a well-intended, but unrealistic, agreement may have repercussions that impact the viability of your Marriage Pact™. Consequently, it's a good idea to recognize this need and plan for the on-going maintenance of your marriage. There are three types of maintenance: Regularly Scheduled Preventive Maintenance, Situational Maintenance and Tune-ups.

REGULARLY SCHEDULED PREVENTIVE MAINTENANCE

It's a good idea to schedule regular reviews of your Marriage Pact. During the first five years of your marriage we suggest you do this annually because things are new and you will undoubtedly need to do some fine tuning. After the first five years, reviewing your agreements every three to five years will be adequate for most couples.

You do not need to review every category, but it is a good idea to review your financial situation annually including goals, spending and saving habits, debt and credit report status. Additionally, each of you should pick at least two other topics where you feel your relationship would benefit from a review and renewed focus.

One of the best things a couple can do from time to time is review the choices they made, both good and bad, that have shaped the current state of their relationship.

Source Unknown

SITUATIONAL MAINTENANCE

When you anticipate making a life-changing move in the near future, it is an excellent idea to review your agreements on that topic before you commit to the change. For example, the time to review your agreements about raising children is before you work on becoming pregnant, not three weeks before the baby is born.

In addition to planning to start a family, any situation that will impact your family if it comes to pass should automatically trigger reviews of related portions of your Marriage Pact". This includes anything that will dramatically impact your income, financial security, free time, time together or life style including:

- buying a home or investment property
- changing jobs
- starting a business
- an upcoming union strike vote
- corporate downsizing that may eliminate your job
- going back to school
- children joining sport teams or taking music lessons

You may discover that you skipped over some of the questions or didn't answer them very completely when the reality of implementing these areas seemed so far in the future. Make plans now. Explore your options. Making plans and working together as a team will give you a sense of power and some degree of control over any situation. This will greatly reduce the stress associated with uncertainty and decision making in your marriage.

TUNE-UPS

Whenever any portion of your marriage isn't working as well as it could be, it's time for a tune-up. Don't delay until you are in crisis. If something has been bugging you, nip the problem in the bud and get it resolved.

When you find that a portion of your Marriage Pact" is not working for you, change it. Use the same process you used to develop your original pact, but limit your discussions to those areas that aren't working as well as expected.

If you have been communicating honestly and openly, problems will be obvious to both of you. Even so, reaching new agreements may not be easy.

Remember, you made a deal. It's not okay for you to decide an agreement isn't working and coerce your partner into accepting your terms. That's a sure way for one of you to lose - which means you both lose. Since any change will impact both of you, you must concur that change is needed and agree on new terms. This is vital to keeping the spirit of your Marriage Pact" and having it work for you.

If you remember that you're a team and focus on working for your mutual benefit, it will be easier to resolve problems. You may find a trade off will make both of you happy. "If you let me off the hook on XYZ, I'll agree not to hold you to ABC."

We generally start by identifying the real issues and then work to resolve them creatively without bloodshed or bruised egos. For example, we originally agreed that I was responsible for cooking and cleaning up the kitchen. Subsequently, we agreed that I would go to night school. This made it very inconvenient to cook and clean on the evenings I went to school. Even so, it was still my responsibility to handle the cooking and keep the kitchen clean because Mike was not willing to take on these duties and we couldn't afford to pay someone to do them.

In working out a solution, we identified time as the issue from my perspective. From Mike's perspective the tasks themselves were the primary issues, but time was also an issue. We resolved it by compromising on the quality of the jobs. Dishes sat in the sink for a couple of days and school night dinners would sometimes be a bowl of cereal or planned leftovers. Mike helped me with other tasks when time allowed so I was free to prepare meals in advance and have more free time to spend with him. Remember, there is no right or wrong solution to a problem.

If you don't like something, change it. If you can't change it, change your attitude. Don't complain.

Maya Angelou

You will face many choices in your relationship. Many couples use these to test each other, requiring their spouses to prove their love, repeatedly. How exhausting!

A well-constructed Marriage Pact" can eliminate much of this push and pull. It gives you guidelines within which to make decisions and you know your rights and obligations. If you've agreed that you will continue in your Thursday bowling league, bowling on

Thursday should neither be a source of hurt feelings nor a bone of contention. As long as the circumstances remain the same, there is really nothing to discuss.

When things change materially, you need to reevaluate your agreement. Let's say your team decides that to stay in the Thursday bowling league you have to commit to practice on Tuesdays. Based on the increase in time and expense this would require, your continued involvement should be renegotiated with your spouse.

You may find that you want to completely change an agreement in your Pact. Our most difficult agreement was that we would not have children. I had wanted children. Mike, who had three children from his first marriage and could not bear the thought, no matter how remote it seemed, that he might lose his children again, was not willing to have another child. After eight years of marriage (with not one word from me on this issue to Mike, or anyone else), Mike decided he would like me to have the experience of being a mother. He brought it up and we changed this agreement. Ironically, since we almost didn't get married because of this agreement, I was unable to have children despite numerous fertility procedures.

If you're not sure you want to permanently make a change, you might allow for a trial period. For example, for my night school/ cooking and cleaning dilemma, we might have agreed that Mike would handle kitchen clean-up for my first semester of night school to help me ease into this program. Whatever you decide, be certain to write out the terms of the trial period to make sure there are no misunderstandings later.

Keep your pact working for you. Taking it for granted or ignoring portions may erode the basis of your relationship.

When you got married you thought it was worth it.

Choose that it's still worth it.

Why wait? Life is not a dress rehearsal.
Quit practicing what you're going to do, and just do it.
In one bold stroke you can transform today.

Marilyn Grey

PART IV

WHERE DO YOU
GO FROM HERE?

Any powerful idea is absolutely fascinating--
and absolutely useless unless we choose to use it.

Richard Bach

NEXT STEPS

INTEGRATE THE CLUES INTO YOUR MARRIAGE

Start with Clue #1 and recommit to each other every day. It is so easy. Once you have that under your belt, add the others.

CREATE YOUR MARRIAGE PACT™

If you haven't yet created an Emotional Prenuptial™ for your relationship, please do. You will be grateful you did this every day for the rest of your lives.

MEET LIKE-MINDED COUPLES

One of the best ways to remain happily married is to spend time with other happily married couples. It is such a delight to be around others who obviously love and respect each other. As we look at the couples we enjoy, there is a wide range of ages, employment, wealth and social standing. Some have young children at home, others are grandparents and even great grandparents. The only common denominator is that we are all happy in our marriages.

It is demoralizing to be around couples who disrespect each other or fight constantly, and it's easy to start picking up some of their bad habits.

SPREAD THE WORD

So, should you dump your old friends if they're no getting along? No. But if their bickering gets in the way of a pleasant evening for all, things need to change. Pass your copy of this book along to them, buy them their own copy or tell them to go online to www.MasteringMarriage.com where they can read the book free of charge.

No, that is not a misprint. We don't want money to be a barrier for individuals to access this guide. If people can't afford to pay for this information or aren't willing to spend their money on it, we will let them read it free. We are committed to strengthening families by helping couples stay happy and in love. Please help spread the word.

JOIN MARRIAGE MASTERS™ - IT'S FREE

Another way to stay connected with like-minded couples is to join Marriage Masters™ at www.MarriageMasters.com. Membership is free, so take advantage of the resources to help you stay happily married. Please come and show your support for marriage by joining our ranks. Your personal information will not be sold or shared with anyone.

Our vision is to make MarriageMasters.com an information and resource hub. It will be "the Web site for happy couples by happy couples™." Our goal is to create a network of committed couples who will share their tips and techniques for staying happy and in love through all the stages of marriage. Our plans include offering money saving and time saving tips so you have more time to spend together and more money to spend or save as well. Some of our specific plans include:

- Bulletin boards by subject area where you can share your successes with couples who will benefit from your experience. For example - if you have children, you know how helpful it would have been to get ideas on how to make time for each other after the baby comes home.
- Rewards for staying married. Our society should celebrate marriage. We will recruit corporate sponsors to donate free and reduce-price products and services to send member couples on their anniversaries. This virtual gift basket will be delivered by MarriageMasters.com via e-mail. Your personal information will be confidential and will not be shared with anyone - not even our sponsors.
- Date ideas for married couples.
- Romantic tip exchange for celebrating special occasions without breaking your budget.
- Vacation ideas for married couples, along with discounts by airlines, hotel chains, rental car companies and cruise lines to make these vacations more affordable.
- A choice of weekly menus ranging from meat and potatoes to vegetarian, complete with recipes, grocery lists and coupons for items featured that week.
- Short-cut tips for household chores.

Please join now and encourage your friends and family to join, too. Help us celebrate marriage.

START A MARRIAGE MASTERS™ GROUP IN YOUR COMMUNITY

If you're someone who likes to make things happen, talk with your clergy or other community leader and see how you might work together to organize activities for Marriage Masters™ in your community. Your local leaders probably already have connections to other couples who want to remain happily married. Getting everyone involved will benefit all of you. There will be an idea exchange for group gatherings posted at the site as well. If you have been part of a group that has successfully held activities for happily married couples, please share your ideas at the Web site - there will be many groups who would love to know what has worked for others.

Help make it fashionable to be "happily married and proud to say so™." The ideas and information provided on the Web site are designed to make your marriage an even greater place to be. Please put them to work for you and the people you care about most.

---

*If you accommodate others,
you will be accommodating yourself.*

Chinese proverb

NOW
IT'S UP TO YOU TWO

Ultimately our concept is simple. You want a fabulous relationship? Then make your relationship fabulous. Know that you make choices when you choose a partner for a lifetime. Work at staying together.

- Choose to be married to each other every day.
- Make your partner #1 in your life.
- Use your power lovingly
- Be the person you "sold" to your partner when you dated.
- Accept your partner "as is."
- Never say no to sex with your spouse.
- Structure your relationship carefully.
- Say what you mean and mean what you say.
- Be sure any conflict is worth the time and energy you put into it.
- Thank your partner for being part of your life.
- Establish an overall financial strategy.
- Create your own secret language of calming cues.

- Say please, thank you and I'm sorry.
- Bend the Golden Rule.
- Develop a selective memory.
- Let your actions say, "I love you."
- Be your spouse's biggest fan.
- Be a team player.
- Remember, most things can just be preferences.
- Create a Marriage Pact™ that is fair to both of you.
- Keep your word.

It doesn't have to be complicated. Keep it simple. Love each other. Be happy with the choices you've made.

It's been said that the bitterest tears cried over graves
are for words never said and deeds never done.
Sad to say, the same holds true for a marriage,
before it's ended by death or by choice.
Make the most of it, before it ends –
and maybe it won't have to end.
Don't hold back –
assume this is the only marriage you'll ever have.

Natalie Schafer

JUST CHECKING

Mr. B, I just want you to know that even though sometimes you've been a real pain in the butt on this project, I still pick you.

Good.

Do you still pick me?

Yes.

Even though I've awakened you dozens of times to tell you some hair-brained idea for this book?

Yes.

Even though you've eaten lots of cereal for dinner because I've been too busy to cook?

Yes.

Even though I've been cranky and irritable and ungroomed and single-minded and sat in front of my computer for hour after hour after hour?

Yes.

So say it.
What?
I want you to say you pick me.
You pick me.
You know what I mean. I want you to say, "I pick you."
I pick you.
Now say it like you mean it this time.
I pick you.
 Really?
Yes. I really pick you. I really, really, really, really pick you. I pick you today, tomorrow and forever.
Hey, you can't do that. You can only pick one day at a time.
Well, let's change the rules.
No way! I want you picking me every day. It makes my heart happy. In fact, I want to hear you say it again right now ...

PART

THE MARRIAGE PACT™ QUESTIONNAIRE

If you have built castles in the air,
your work need not be lost.
That is where they should be.
Now put the foundation under them.

Henry David Thoreau

THE MARRIAGE PACT™ QUESTIONNAIRE

You may have heard this line from *Auntie Mame* by Patrick Dennis, "Life is a banquet, and most poor suckers are starving to death." Creating your Marriage Pact™ is your ticket to life's main course - marriage.

Consciously formulating your Marriage Pact™ is key to staying happy and in love. Take advantage of this amazing opportunity to get to know yourself and your spouse. It will have a profound impact on your future together.

You are going to be so happy you did this.

Bon Appetit!

You will come to know that what appears today
to be a sacrifice will prove instead
to be the greatest investment that you will ever make.

Gorden B. Hinkley

NOTES:

1. When a question includes "you/spouse," answer the question for yourself as well as what you think the answer is for your spouse. For example, for the question, "Do you/spouse smoke?" You would answer twice. I would answer this question, "No, I don't smoke and neither does Mike."

2. If you prefer the convenience of a write-in workbook or completing this information on-line, please see page 252 for information on alternative questionnaire formats.

ABOUT ME
Full Name
Nickname(s)
City, State, Country of Birth
Height, Weight, Hair Color, Eye Color
Birth Date, Astrological Sign, Date We Met
What are your sizes, favorite brands and favorite colors of: Shoes?
    Socks? Hat? Gloves? Pants (waist, inseam)? Shirt (neck, sleeve
    length)? Dress? Skirt? Bra? Hose?
Social Security Number, Driver's License Number
Mother's Maiden Name, Married Name, Phone, Address
Father's Name, Phone, Address

AFFECTION
What non-sexual ways do you like to be touched?
Are there any ways that you do not like to be touched?
Do you like to hold hands in public?
Do you like to hug in public?
Do you like to kiss in public?
When is it inappropriate to show affection?
Is it OK for your spouse to ask you to be hugged?
How many hugs do you like/need in a day?
If your spouse wants to hold hands, be hugged, etc. how should he let
    you know?
Do you plan to hug, kiss, hold hands with, put your arm around
    anyone other than your spouse once you are married? If yes,
    with whom will you do these things?
If your affection to others causes your spouse to be jealous, how
    should he tell you?
Will you stop doing whatever is causing your spouse to be jealous?

ALCOHOL & DRUGS

Do you/spouse drink alcoholic beverages?

Have you/spouse consumed alcoholic beverages in the past?

Do you/spouse use recreational drugs?

Have you/spouse used recreational drugs in the past? If yes, what kinds of drugs? How often?

What problems has your drinking or drug use ever caused?

Has drinking or drug use ever caused you to miss work?

Have you been arrested because of drinking/drug use?

Have you ever been involved with Alcoholics Anonymous or other support group for users?

Do you mind if others drink?

Do you mind if others do recreational drugs?

Will guests be allowed to drink in your home? Do drugs?

If you feel strongly against alcohol or doing drugs, do you ever find it acceptable? If yes, what types of drugs or alcohol might be acceptable? When would these be acceptable?

Are you currently taking any prescription drugs? Are any of these optional? If you can't stop, why not?

What role do you want your spouse to play if she sees you becoming dependent on drugs or alcohol?

What role do you want to play if you see your spouse getting into trouble with drugs or alcohol?

Who will abstain and be the designated driver when you drink or do drugs away from home?

If you/spouse drink or do drugs, will you/spouse stop during pregnancy? When trying to conceive? After children are born?

BAD HABITS

What are your odd or bad habits? What things about you have driven your parents, siblings, friends and former roommates crazy?

Are you trying to break a bad habit at this time? What bad habit(s)?

Is there anything you would like your partner to do to help you accomplish this goal?

BIRTH CONTROL

Does your religion place restrictions on birth control or abortion? If yes, what are they?

Will you use birth control? If yes, what form? What risks are associated with this form? Are there other forms you would consider using?

Would you consider being sterilized after you have children? Would your consider sterilization for your spouse?

What will you do if you become pregnant in spite of birth control?

What are your views on abortion? Would you ever consider an abortion for you/spouse? If yes, under what circumstances? How late in pregnancy?

CALMING CUES

Are there any existing situations in your relationship that would benefit from a calming cue? What is the trigger? What cue could you use? What should each of you do once a calming cue has been given?

CHILDREN

EVERYONE should complete the CHILDREN - BASICS section. If you have or are considering having children, answer all questions in the Children section.

CHILDREN - ADULT CHILDREN (OVER AGE 18)

Do you have children over the age of 18? If yes, what is your relationship with them? What is your spouse's relationship with them?

Do your adult children live with you? If yes, why? How long do you expect them to live with you?

Under what circumstances would you be willing to have adult children live with you? Illness? Financial trouble? Marriage problems? They need help raising their children/your grandchildren?

How long would you allow them to live with you?

Do you believe that adult children who live with their parents should pay for room and board? If yes, how much? If no, why not?

If your adult children were to live at home, who would do their laundry? Pay for dry cleaning? Prepare meals? Clean their room? Provide them with a car? Pay for their car insurance? Pay their phone bills? Provide them with spending money? Pay for health insurance? Pay their medical bills?

Would you ever move to be closer to adult children? If no, would you move to be further away from adult children?

Would you give financial support to your adult children not living with you? Under what circumstances? How much? How long?

Would you lend your adult children money? For what purpose? How much? For how long? Would you expect them to pay you back? Would you charge interest? Would you have them sign a loan document? Would you foreclose on a loan to your child?

Whose opinion will matter more to you, your adult child's or your spouse's?

CHILDREN - BASICS

Do you like children? Do you have any children? If yes, how many? What ages? Do you want to have (more) children? If yes, how

CHILDREN - BASICS, cont.

many children? When would you like to start a family?

What's your favorite age child? What's your least favorite age child?

Would you like to have a son(s)? Daughter(s) Would you like to follow practices designed to improve your chances of having the gender you prefer?

Would you consider genetic screening for birth defects?

How do you feel about being a parent? What will you do best as a parent? What will you do least well as a parent?

CHILDREN - CHORES

What chores will your children be expected to do? At what age? Examples: set table, clear table, load dishwasher, wash dishes, make own bed, clean own room, clean house, make own snack, make own lunch, cook for family, do own laundry, do family laundry, iron own clothes, iron for family, take out trash, help with yard, mow grass, rake leaves, wash family car, grocery shop, run errands, tutor siblings, baby-sit siblings.

If children will not be expected to do chores, how will you teach them the associated skills and responsibility?

What action will you take if a child refuses (or conveniently forgets) to do her chores?

Will you pay them to do their chores? If yes, how much will you pay them? If no, how will they learn the correlation between work and income?

Will you expect your children to get jobs? If yes, at what age? What types of jobs are acceptable? Baby-sitting, newspaper route, lawn mowing, bus boy, waitress, fast food worker, golf caddy, model? At what age? If "no" Why not?

How may children use their earnings? Of every (after tax) dollar children earn, what percent should they save for short term

CHILDREN - CHORES, cont.

goals (toy, book, gifts)? Save for long term goals (college, car)? Give to charity? Contribute to family or expenses? Pay their debts? Use as they please? (Total should be 100%)

NOTE You are establishing habits that will last your child's lifetime. We urge you to start your children saving now. Set up separate savings accounts, piggy banks or envelopes so that your children gain the experience of making choices about spending and savings.

CHILDREN - CULTURALIZATION

Whose family customs will you follow daily? Whose family customs will you follow at holidays? What are these customs?

What nationality will your children be?

What language(s) will your children speak at home? What language(s) will your children speak at school?

What religion will your children follow? Will your children attend religious services? If yes, how often will they attend religious services? Will your children receive religious education? If yes, what religious education will your children receive?

Will your children be baptized/dedicated? If yes, at what age? Will your children have a Bar/Bat Mitzvah? Will your children be confirmed? If yes, at what age? Does this differ from what your family wants or expects for your children? If yes, how does it differ?

If your differences of opinion cause problems with your family, will you change your plans for your child? If yes, how?

Whose feelings matter more to you on this issue, your partner's or your family's?

CHILDREN - DAILY CARE

Will you/spouse work outside the home after the baby is born? If yes, how soon after baby's birth? Who will take care of baby while you/spouse work?

Will your baby be breast fed? If yes, for how many months do you expect to breast feed?

Who will change diapers? Who will dress baby? Who will feed baby? Who will give middle of the night feedings?

Who will take care of children on weekday evenings? Who will take care of children on weekends?

Is it okay for boys and girls to share a bedroom? If yes, until what age?

CHILDREN - DISCIPLINE

Who will discipline your children? How will your children be disciplined? Will you ever spank them? If yes, under what circumstances will you spank them? Who will spank them?

How much leeway should children have before they are disciplined verbally? How much leeway should children have before they are disciplined physically?

Will your parents or others be allowed to discipline your children? If so, who may discipline your children? How will your parents or others be allowed to discipline your children?

Will boys and girls be disciplined the same? If not, how will their disciplines differ?

What bedtimes and curfews will you set for your children as Toddlers (ages 1-2), Preschool (3-5), Grade School (6-11), Jr. High (12-13) High School (14-18)? College/Trade School living at home, done with education and living at home, returning home after divorce?

CHILDREN-EDUCATION

Will your children go to day care? If yes, at what age? Where?

For kindergarten through high school, will your children go to public or private schools? Is there a particular public or private school you want them to attend? If yes, what is it?

Do you want your children to go to college? If yes, do you have a school in mind that you hope they will attend?

When and how will you save to pay for private school or college?

CHILDREN - ENTERTAINMENT

What kinds of things do you see yourself/spouse doing with your children? Will you play together? If yes, what kinds of things will you do?

Will your children go with you when you go out or will you hire a sitter? How old will your children be when you first leave them with a baby sitter? Who will baby-sit for your children?

Will you take vacations with or without the children?

Will you restrict your children to age-appropriate activities or let them do grown-up things? (e.g., take young children to see R-rated movies, wear make-up at a young age)

How much TV should children watch each day? Who will monitor acceptability of TV shows?

Will you read to your children? Who will read to them? How often will you read to them? When will you read to them?

To what types of music will you expose your child? Not allow?

CHILDREN - EXPECTATIONS

What do you expect of your children in general? Any scholastic, athletic, social or career expectations?

List any sports you hope they play. List any sports you do not want them to play. Why?

CHILDREN-EXPECTATIONS, cont.

Will your child play a musical instrument? If yes, which one would you prefer?

What if your child doesn't want or like what you had hoped for?

CHILDREN - LIFE SKILLS

Who will teach your children their life skills? i.e., How to make bed, clean room, yard work, wash car, do laundry, cook, dress, bathe, make repairs, manage money, sports, reading, writing, math, use computer, manners, negotiating, conflict resolution?

Will you tell your children how you as a couple resolve differences? Make decisions? Spend money? Set priorities? If yes, at what age?

How will you teach children responsibility? How to handle peer pressure? Make decisions? Keep their word? Values? Morals?

CHILDREN - MEDICAL

Is there a family history of twins, birth defects, retardation or problem pregnancies? If yes, describe.

Any reason you may not be able to have children?

If you are unable to bear children, would you consider artificial insemination? *In vitro* fertilization? A surrogate mother? Adoption? If you would consider adopting, any limits on child's race, health, sex, age, heritage? Foster parenting?

Have you ever been pregnant or made someone pregnant? Have you ever miscarried? Have you ever had an abortion? Have you ever relinquished a child for adoption?

CHILDREN - NAMES

Are there special names you want to name your children? If yes, what are they?

What surname will your children be given?

CHILDREN - PARENT TIME

How will you make time for each other after you have children:
Right after birth? Toddler? School age? Older?

CHILDREN - PROBLEMS

Do you have any reason to suspect that you may not be a fit parent?
Do you have any reason to suspect that you might physically
abuse your child? Do you have the patience to be a parent?

Will you disagree or argue in front of your children?

What would you do if you discover your child is using drugs? Having
sex? Missing school? Stealing? Fighting? Lying? Cheating?

Would you consider getting professional help/family counseling?
Why or why not?

CHILDREN - SOCIAL DEVELOPMENT

At what age should children wear make-up? Begin dating? Get
pierced ears? Wear adult-style clothing? Own a car?

Should children be taught about sex? Contraception? Disease
prevention? If yes, at what age? Who should teach them?

What will you do or not do to foster self-esteem?

How will your child address you and your spouse? Your parents?
Your siblings? Adults in general? Relatives? Adult friends?

What extra curricular activities do you anticipate for your children?
Girl Scouts? Karate? Soccer? Drama club? Ballet? Other?

CHILDREN - STEPCHILDREN

How many are there? What ages are they? How well do you get along
with them? If you have children, how well do your children get
along with partner's children?

How do you feel about your stepchildren?

Where will they live? How often will you see them?

CHILDREN-STEPCHILDREN, cont.

Who will discipline them?

Who will pay for stepchildren's child support? College expenses? Weddings? Visits? Joint vacations?

Who will communicate with the children's other parent?

What relationship will children have with natural grandparents? What relationship will children have with step grandparents?

What will they call their stepparent? Step grandparents?

Would the stepparent like to legally adopt them?

CHILDREN - YOUR CHILDHOOD

Who raised you? Was your household male or female dominant?

What was your home life like? What responsibilities did you have at home? How did you feel about them? Do you want your children to have more, less or same amount of responsibility?

In what school/community activities did you participate? What/who were important influences in your upbringing?

What did your parents do best as parents? Least well as parents?

What specific things did your parents do in raising you that you want to do in raising your children? What specific things did your parents do in raising you that you do not want to do when raising your children?

CITIZENSHIP

What is your citizenship?

Do you donate time to community activities? If yes, how much time per month? If yes, to what groups?

Do you donate time to charitable groups? If yes, how much time per month? If yes, to what groups?

Are you patriotic? What does this mean to you?

What are your views on military service?

COMMITMENT

Will you recommit to your marriage every day? How or what words will you use?

What things or people may take precedence over your spouse once in a while? Work? Family? Children? How should your spouse approach this subject if they feel that "once in a while" is becoming excessive?

COMMUNICATIONS

Are you a talker or the quiet type? If there is a pause in the conversation, are you likely to fill it? How do you feel about quiet people/talkers (whichever is unlike you)?

When do you like to talk? Are there times when you like to be left alone?

If your partner needs to talk and feels you aren't listening, what should she do to get your full attention? When and where should she approach you? Not approach you?

When you have something important to discuss, do you communicate best verbally or in writing? If one of you prefers verbal and the other written communication, how will you communicate?

Where do you like to have a good talk? Any places you don't want to talk seriously (e.g., in bed, during meals, while watching TV)?

What do you like to talk about? What will be difficult for you to discuss? Are there any subjects you prefer not to discuss? If yes, which ones?

DEATH

When you die, do you want to be buried or cremated? Where would you like to be buried, or what should be done with your ashes?

Do you want to donate your organs? If yes, are you donating all

DEATH, cont.

organs? If not all organs, which ones?

What type of service should be held in your honor? Religious service? Memorial service at funeral home? Wake? Party? Nothing?

Do you want a big budget or economy funeral?

Do you expect that your wishes are at odds with those of your family? If yes, explain. If there's a disagreement, should your spouse give in to family pressures? How strongly do you feel about this?

How long after your death should your partner wait to date?

How long after your death should your partner wait to remarry?

Do you have a will? If yes, where is it? What are the general terms of your will? Will you make a new will when you marry? If yes, what will the new terms be?

Do you have burial insurance? If yes, where is this policy?

Do you have a life insurance policy? If yes, who is the beneficiary? Will spouse be beneficiary when you marry? If no, why not?

DECISION MAKING

How will you choose who gets to decide on all the little things that come up (e.g., which restaurant you'll go to, who will be invited to a party, how dressed up you'll get for the party at Smith's, what to buy for someone's birthday, which TV show to watch)?

How will you resolve disagreements on major issues (e.g., will you buy a new car or fix your present car, what style furniture to buy, will you take a European vacation or make a down payment on a house . . .)?

How do you see your marriage being structured? Dictatorship? Kingdom? Democracy? Day to day decisions? Major decisions?

If your choose a democracy, how will you decide what to do when you have a tie vote?

ECOLOGY/ THE ENVIRONMENT

How important is ecology/the environment to you?

Are you involved in any ecology/environmental efforts at this time? If yes, which ones? How much time do you currently devote to these efforts each month?

Do you want to be more involved in ecology issues? If yes, how much time do you want to devote?

Do you recycle? Will you recycle? What do/will you recycle?

If you have children, will you use disposable diapers?

Will you use Styrofoam containers?

Would you buy an electric or hybrid car?

EDUCATION

What is the highest level of education you have completed?

Do you have all the education you want to have? Explain.

If you plan to go on to school, what will your education cost? How will you pay for it? How long will it take for your expected increase in income to cover the cost of your education?

If you both want to go to school, will you go at the same time or who gets to go first? When does the other person get to go?

For what degree or certificate are you aiming? If your spouse works to put you through school, does he have a right to feel he should receive part of your income for life should you divorce? Why or why not?

Are you interested in taking adult education or other non-degree courses? If yes, what subjects?

EMOTIONS

What do you do when you are angry? How do you want your spouse to react to your anger?

How do you fight? What can your spouse do to avoid a fight?

EMOTIONS, cont.

Are you good at forgiving and forgetting? What can you do to become a more forgiving *and* forgetting person?

What do you do when you are being selfish? Unreasonable? Hurt? Sad? Depressed?

How would you like your spouse to treat you when you are being selfish? Unreasonable? Hurt? Sad? Depressed?

What can your spouse do to show his emotional support?

What do you do to relax or shake off the blahs?

What do you do when you're happy? What makes you happy?

What are you afraid of? What do you do when you're frightened?

EMPLOYMENT

Do you work? If yes, for whom? What kind of work do you do? How do you get to work? Will you continue to work in this same job when you get married? What employee benefits do you get?

Are you in a union? If yes, what is the strike history? How do strikes affect you? When is your contract renegotiated? Is a strike likely? During a strike, what income do you have? Will you seek other employment to supplement your income when you are on strike? Do you expect your spouse to seek extra employment to help cover expenses during your strike?

Does your spouse work? If yes, for whom? What kind of work does your spouse do? How does your spouse get to work? Will your spouse continue to work in this same job when you marry?

Is your spouse in a union? If yes, what is the strike history? How do strikes affect your spouse? When is his contract renegotiated? Is a strike likely? During a strike, what income does he have? Will your spouse seek other employment to supplement your income when your spouse is on strike? Do you expect to seek extra employment to help cover expenses during his strikes?

EMPLOYMENT, CONT.

What hours are you scheduled to work? How much overtime do you generally work? When is overtime most likely? Are you paid straight salary, commission, hourly or a combination?

Do you travel for your job? If no, would you be willing to travel? How often? If yes, where do you travel? How often? How long are you gone? Could your spouse travel with you? What if your spouse wants you to find a job that requires less travel?

Are you willing to have your spouse take a job that requires travel? How much travel would be acceptable to you?

What do you like about your job? What are the drawbacks?

How happy are you with your current job?

Would you like to change jobs? If yes, explain.

Is a promotion for you likely to require relocation? Are you willing to relocate for a promotion?

Is a promotion for your partner likely to require relocation? Are you willing to relocate for your partner's promotion?

What happens if your spouse must relocate to find a job and you are very happy with your job?

What is your career objective? What are your job dreams/fantasies?

How will you feel if your spouse's career progresses faster than yours? Slower than yours?

How do you feel about your spouse's time commitment for career success? How do you think your spouse feels about your time commitment for success?

Do either of your families have a business they hope you/spouse will become involved in? If yes, explain. Does the family business appeal to you? Do you feel you must join the family business? Do you feel your spouse must join the family business?

Is it okay for you/spouse to take a cut in pay to take a job that offers more personal satisfaction?

Are there any family expectations?

EMPLOYMENT, cont.

Do you ever hope to start your own business? If yes, doing what? Why don't you start your business now?

If your spouse wanted to mortgage your home to start a business, would that be okay with you? Would you be willing to mortgage your home to start your dream business?

How important to you are company benefits like health and life insurance, dental plan, retirement plan?

Have you ever been fired or laid off? If yes, explain.

If you were to be fired tomorrow, how would you cope with financial obligations? The emotional aftermath? Would you consider seeing an employment counselor to help you find a new job? A mental health counselor should you experience depression or anxiety if you lose your job?

How would you want spouse to react to your being fired? Laid off?

FAMILY & IN-LAWS

What is your relationship with your family? What is your relationship with your spouse's family?

What relationship do you want your spouse to have with your family? What relationship do you hope to develop with your in-laws?

Have your families met? If yes, do they get along? If no, do you think they will get along?

How often do you see or talk to your family now? How often will you see or talk to your family once you're married?

How often do you see or talk to spouse's family now? How often will you see or talk to your spouse's family once you're married?

Will you visit parents and relatives separately or together?

Do you count on your family for money? Will they continue to give you money when you marry?

FAMILY & IN-LAWS, cont.

Do you stand to inherit a significant amount of money or possessions? How far in the future?

Does your family count on you for money? Health care assistance? Companionship? Grandchildren? How do you plan to meet these needs in your marriage?

Have you talked openly with your family about how your marriage will affect your relationship with them? Will you talk about this before your wedding? If yes, will you talk to them by yourself or will your partner be with you for this conversation?

How far away do you live from your relatives? How far away do you live from your spouse's relatives? How do you feel about the distance you live from your families?

Would you ever turn down a job opportunity because it would cause you to move too far away from or too close to family or relatives? If yes, explain.

What's the farthest you've ever been from home? What's the longest time you've been away from your family? What's the longest time you'd ever want to be away from your family?

FAMILY MEMBERS WITH SPECIAL NEEDS

Note: Special needs include physical, mental and emotional limitations that require modifications to, or assistance with, day to day tasks that most of us take for granted. The cause may be genetic or result from birth trauma, stroke, illness, accident or age.

Do you have any relatives with special needs? If yes, who are these people and what special needs do they have? What is your current relationship with them? What would you like your relationship with them to be?

If a family member developed a special need, would you be willing to have him live with you? If yes, what level of care would you be

FAMILY MEMBERS WITH SPECIAL NEEDS, cont.

willing and able to provide? Which relatives?

Would you be willing to provide a special needs relative with financial support? If yes, how much and what type of support would you be willing to provide? For how long? Which relatives?

How strong is your commitment to help your special needs relatives?

FINANCES

Have you ever been financially independent? If yes, when? Did you live within your means or go into debt during this time?

How important is money to you? Is it more important to you to look like you have money or actually have money? Are you willing to curtail your spending today to strengthen your financial future?

What sources of income do you have? Your partner?

How much will you earn this year? Your partner?

Will your income change when you marry? If yes, explain.

Once you marry, will you combine all income and consider it equally both of yours? If not, how will you decide whose money it is?

Do you have credit cards? Checking account? Savings account? Credit union account? What are your balances for each? Will you maintain separate and/or joint bank accounts?

Will you maintain separate and/or joint credit cards?

If you maintain separate bank and credit card accounts, what expenses will be paid from each?

IF YOU HAVE ASSETS YOU WANT PROTECTED, YOU NEED A LEGAL DOCUMENT. SEE AN ATTORNEY BEFORE YOU MARRY. *IF YOU ARE ALREADY MARRIED, SEE AN ATTORNEY AS SOON AS POSSIBLE TO SEE WHAT PROTECTION YOU CAN BE AFFORDED.*

Do you like to make safe investments or take financial risks? Under what circumstances would you risk everything you own?

Who will keep track of bills? Write checks? Do your taxes?

What debts and on-going financial commitments do you have?

FINANCES, CONT.

Are you paying or supposed to be paying child support? Parent support? Alimony? Student loans? Car loan/lease? Medical bills? Credit card debt? Other loans? What amounts for each?

How much will you donate to your church-which one? Charity-which charities? Community programs-which ones? Political causes or candidates-which ones? Ecology groups-which ones?

Have you ever had bad credit? Have you ever been turned down for a loan or credit card? Have you ever been bankrupt? If yes, why?

How much do you expect to earn five years from now? What income, in today's dollars, would make you happy? What is the most money you think you'll ever make in a year?

How much spending money will each of you have weekly? What expenses must be covered by this money? (i.e., cigarettes, magazines, impulse shopping, hair cut, gum, lunches, snacks, hobby)

At what dollar value will you discuss a purchase before making it? How will you decide if you will make a particular purchase over the amount at which you agreed to discuss? What will you do if you can't agree on a purchase?

What items over $5,000 do you aspire to own?

What quality will you buy for yourself? Spouse? Children? Home?

How much do you spend on a typical casual outfit? Business outfit? Pair of shoes? Typical accessories?

Do you buy or lease your vehicles? Why?

How much do you currently spend each month on alcohol? Books? Car insurance? Car/truck/vehicle payments? Car maintenance? Cell phone? Clothing? Credit card debt? Decorating? Drugs? Eating out? Entertaining? Entertainment? Gambling? Games? Gifts? Groceries? Health insurance? Hobbies? Home phone? Impulse shopping? Life insurance? Loans? Long distance calls? Pets? Recreation? Rent/mortgage? Student loans? Vacations?

FINANCES, CONT.

Video arcade or pay to play on-line games? Will your spending habits change when you marry? How?

How much do you save monthly? What are you saving for? Will your saving habits change when you get married? If yes, how?

Buying on credit means you don't pay off your full balance each month, not just that you used a credit card for the purchase. How do you use credit? What do you buy on credit? Auto? Clothing? Dating expenses? Education? Entertainment? Food? Games/recreation? Gas? Hobbies? Household items? Furniture? Medical? Travel? Vacations? Will your use of credit change once you marry? If yes, how? What is NOT acceptable for you to buy on credit?

Do you currently have a budget? What items are in your budget? Do you expect to use a budget once married? Who will prepare the budget? How closely do you expect to follow this budget?

Will you voluntarily roll back your lifestyle if ill-fortune and financial disaster hit, or will you wait until you are forced to? If you will voluntarily roll back your expenses, where will you begin?

FITNESS

Is fitness important to you? How do you rate your personal fitness? What would you like your fitness level to be? What are you willing to do to change your fitness level?

What exercise do you do regularly? Do you play any sports? If yes, what sports? How often do you play them?

Can your partner participate in your fitness routine? If yes, how? What can your spouse do to support your fitness efforts? What should your spouse do if he notices your physical condition deteriorating from its current level?

Are you happy with your weight? If not, what can your partner do to support your efforts to lose (gain) weight?

FITNESS, cont.

Have you weighed ten pounds more than you do now? If yes, when?

How would you feel if you gained a great deal of weight after you marry? How would you feel if your spouse gained a great deal of weight after you marry? What should your spouse do or say if they notice you are gaining weight?

FOOD

What are your favorite foods? What food allergies, strong dislikes or taboos do you have? Do you like to try new foods?

Do you like to eat fish? Meat? Seafood? Salad? Vegetables? Dessert? Chinese? Dim sum? Indian? Italian? Japanese? Mexican? Sushi? Thai? What other types do you enjoy/dislike?

How many meals do you eat each day? When do you snack?

What do you typically eat for breakfast? Lunch? Dinner? Snacks?

Who will do the cooking when you marry? When you cook, do you like anyone else in the kitchen? How good a cook are you?

Have you ever had anorexia nervosa? Have you ever suffered from bulimia? Have you ever been a binge eater?

Do you consider your anorexia nervosa, bulimia, or binge eating a problem? If yes, what are you doing about it? How can your spouse help you address this problem?

FRIENDS

Do you feel you can retain separate friends after you marry?

Do you plan to develop friendships as a couple with other couples?

Once you are married, can you have friends of the opposite sex? Can your partner have friends of the opposite sex?

If your partner becomes jealous of your friendship with someone of the opposite sex, will you stop seeing and talking with this person?

If your partner feels you spend too much time with a friend, will you

FRIENDS, cont.

reduce the time you spend with that person?

Do you plan to stop seeing any of your friends after you're married? If yes, which ones? Why will you stop seeing them?

Are there any of your spouse's friends you expect your spouse to stop seeing after marriage? If yes, whom and why?

What ongoing commitments do you have (e.g., team sports, clubs, alumni group, business organizations)? How many nights a week do you plan to spend with friends without your spouse? What will you do when you're with these people?

Can your spouse become involved in your activities with your friends? If yes, how? How many nights a week do you plan to spend with your spouse and friends together?

How many nights a week do you plan to spend alone with your spouse?

GIFTS

Do you expect to give/get an engagement ring? If yes, describe what you'd like. What is a reasonable amount to spend?

For which occasions do you expect to receive gifts? What type of gifts do you want to receive from your spouse? Any type of gifts you do NOT want to receive from your spouse? If yes, explain.

What little gifts might your spouse buy you just to say I love you?

What is a fabulous big gift your spouse could buy you someday?

Do you like to give gifts you have made? Do you like to receive home-made/handmade gifts?

What type of gifts do you want to receive from your children? Are there any types of gifts you do not want to receive from your children? If yes, explain. At what age will children be expected to pay for the gifts they give?

For which occasions will you buy gifts for your children? How much will you spend per occasion when your children are infants? In

GIFTS, cont.

preschool? Grade school? High School? College? Adults?

Will you restrict your gift-buying for your children to the special occasions you listed above?? When the child asks for them? Because you feel like it? If yes, how often and how much will you spend? Who else may buy your children gifts? Will you restrict quantity, content or value of gifts from others? If yes, what restrictions do you envision?

To whom and for what occasions do you give gifts? Who will be responsible for buying gifts for family and friends? To whom will you give gifts once you get married? For what occasions?

GOALS

Is there anything that you've always wanted to do? If yes, what is it?

What are your life dreams or non-sexual fantasies?

Do you have a goal you want to achieve? How can your partner help you achieve these goals?

HEALTH

Do you feel you are in good health now? What health problems do you have or have you had? Anything special you need to do or avoid doing because of your health?

Do you have any blood relatives with heart disease, diabetes, cancer, alcoholism, stroke, sickle cell anemia, allergies or other health problem which might indicate you're at risk? If yes, explain.

What are you doing to minimize your health risks? What can your spouse do to support your efforts to maintain good health?

What blood type are you? Is your blood Rh+ or Rh-?

Do you have health insurance? If yes, with whom? If yes, will your spouse be covered once you marry?

HERITAGE & CULTURE

What is your cultural heritage? What role did this play in your upbringing? What role does it play in your life today?

What languages were spoken in your home? What languages do you speak? What languages do you understand?

Do any of your relatives not speak English? If yes, which ones?

What are your prejudices regarding race? Religion? Skin color? Creed? Education/intelligence? Physical attributes? Manners/social skills? Accents/language/vocabulary? Where someone lives in your city or town? Parts of the country? Foreign countries? Foreign visitors? Immigrants? Illegal immigrants?

HOBBIES

What are your hobbies? How much time do you spend on each hobby each month? How much time would you like to be able to spend on each hobby each month? How much time do you expect to spend on each hobby each month once you are married? Do you want your spouse to participate in your hobbies? If yes, how?

What are your spouse's hobbies? How much time and money do you think your partner currently spends on each hobby each month? How much time and money do you feel your partner should spend on each hobby each month once you are married? Do you want to participate in spouse's hobbies? If yes, how?

HOLIDAYS

Do you get time off at holidays? If yes, which ones?

Which holidays are important to you? How do you currently spend these holidays? Where do you want to spend these holidays, once you're married? With whom do you want to spend the holidays once you're married? After you have children?

230

HOLIDAYS, cont.

When conflicts arise, how will you decide where you'll go or who will join you for holidays?

Would you consider celebrating a holiday early or late in order to be with family or friends?

HOME

Have you ever lived on your own? If yes, when? For how long?

Where will you live initially? Where do you aspire to live?

Will you rent or buy your home at this time? Do you hope to buy in the future? If yes, when? What sacrifices are you willing to make to own your residence?

Would you like to live in an apartment? Co-op? Condo? House? Mobile home? Town house?

When you merge households, what furniture, decorations or other items do you want to move into your combined residence?

What style of furniture would be in your ideal home? Art work? Decorative items? What type of architecture would it be?

What size home would you like to have?

Do you want a second home? If yes, where? When?

Are there places in the home or possessions you want to retain as strictly yours when you're married?

Will anyone other than your spouse and children live with you? If yes, who? Under what conditions would you allow others to live with you?

HOME MAINTENANCE

What types of home maintenance will you do? What types do you expect your spouse to do? What will you pay others to do?

What home maintenance skills do you have? Do you plan to learn any additional skills? If yes, which ones?

Don't worry if your friends aren't comfortable with your agreements. They don't have to live with them.

HOUSEHOLD CHORES

What level of cleanliness do you expect? How often will you vacuum? Dust? Wash floors? Wash windows? Do laundry?

Who will do the following? Pick up of house? Regular cleaning? Heavy cleaning? Grocery shopping? Your clothes shopping? Spouse's clothes shopping? Children's clothes shopping? Take out trash? Laundry? Ironing? Yard work? Make bed? Change sheets? Change light bulbs? Bring in paper? Get mail?

What chores do you currently do for yourself or have others do for you that you expect your spouse to do when you marry?

ILLNESS & INJURY

Should your spouse comfort you or ignore minor accidents and illnesses?

What should your spouse do in the event of a medical emergency? Besides family, whom should he contact?

If there is no hope for your recovery from illness or accident and you will be a vegetable, should extraordinary measures be taken to keep you alive?

If your illness were not covered by insurance, how much of your own money would you spend to try and save your life if you thought you could recover completely? If you thought you'd be mentally competent but physically paralyzed? If you'd be a vegetable?

If your spouse's illness were not covered by insurance, how much of your own money would you spend to try and save your spouse's life if you thought spouse could recover completely? If you thought spouse would be mentally competent but physically paralyzed? If you thought spouse would be a vegetable?

If you have not yet done so, see a lawyer to create a living will and durable power of attorney so that your wishes are followed in the event of your incapacitation - which can happen in an instant.

LEISURE PURSUITS

What sports do you like to watch? How often?

Do you keep abreast of current events? If yes, how?

What magazines, newspapers, types of books do you read?

Are you a skilled dancer? Do you like to dance? What dances do you enjoy? Will you dance to please your partner? How often?

What types of music do you enjoy? How often? Any types of music you can't stand? If yes, what types? Do you like background music or do you only play music when you focus on it?

What card games do you enjoy playing? How often? Do you belong to a card, dominos, mahjong, bingo or other club? If no, would you like to? Which board games do you enjoy?

Do you know how to play bridge? Poker? Domino's? Bingo? Do you play these or other games for money?

How do you feel about gambling? Do you like to gamble/play games of chance? Do you play the lottery? Bet at the track? Play the slots? Go to casinos? Bet on sport events? What other gambling do you do?

Do you prefer staying home or going out? How often do you like to go out? What do you like to do when you go out? Do you like to get dressed up or prefer casual attire when you go out? Define dressed up and casual.

During which times, meals or events is it important that you and your spouse be at home? During which times, meals or events is it important that you and your spouse be out on the town?

Do you like to go to parties? What types do you enjoy? Do you like to give parties? What types do you enjoy giving? How many people would be at your ideal party?

How often do you currently entertain? Where do you entertain?

LEISURE PURSUITS, cont.

Home? Club? Restaurant? Will the frequency or where you entertain change when you marry? If yes, how?

How many hours is the TV on in your home each day? How many hours do you watch TV a day? In what room(s) do you watch TV? What are your favorite shows to watch? What types of shows do you dislike? Do you plan to change your TV viewing habits once you're married? If yes, how?

How often do you go to the movies? How often would you like to go to the movies? Do you watch movies on TV (this includes movies on video, DVD, pay per view, made for TV movies, etc.)? How many videos, DVD's, pay per view, or made for TV movies do you watch each week?

Do you play video games, arcade games or computer games? If yes, how many hours do you play each day? Do you play alone? If no, whom do you play against? Do you plan to change your video game playing habits once you're married? If yes, how?

How much time do you spend at home on the computer? How do you spend your time on the computer? (i.e., working, answering e-mail, searching the web, shopping, chat rooms) Do you plan to change the amount of time you spend on the computer once you're married? If yes, how?

NAMES

What is the name you were given at birth? What is your legal name now? What nicknames or aliases have you used in the past or currently use? What would you like your legal name to be upon your marriage? Spouse's legal name?

If your partner wants to join both your last names so that both of you take on new names when you marry (such as Jane Hanson and

NAMES, cont.

Fred Smith becoming Jane Hanson-Smith and Fred Hanson-Smith), would you consider this?

What names do you like being called? What name do you prefer your spouse call you?

Are there any pet names your spouse calls you that you want used only when the two of you are alone?

List any names people call you that you dislike.

PET PEEVES

What things drive you crazy in general? (Remember, this is not about making your partner over. It's okay to say that a messy house drives you crazy, but not okay to say that your partner's sloppiness drives you crazy. Once identified, each of you may see things you can do so that your actions don't aggravate the other's pet peeves.)

What things about your parents or relatives drive you crazy?

Are you afraid you're going to do some of these things yourself? If yes, which ones?

What do you want your spouse to do if you start picking up some of these irritating habits?

PETS

Do you have any pets? If yes, list how many, the variety and the names of your pets. How much time does it take each day to feed, exercise, clean-up after and otherwise care for them?

If you don't have a pet, do you want a pet? If yes, how many and what kind of pet would you like?

How many and what kinds of pets does your spouse have? What if both of you have pets and they don't get along?

PETS, cont.

Who takes care of your pet now? When you get married, who will take care of your pet? What will you do with your pet when you and spouse are gone for a day? For an extended period?

Where will your pet stay during the day when you are at home? During the day when you are not at home? At night? Do any of your pets currently share your bed with you? Do you expect your pets to share your bed when you get married? If your pet has been sharing your bed and you don't plan to allow your pet to share your bed once you are married, will you give in and let the pet on the bed if it seems unhappy with this new arrangement?

How much money would you be willing to spend to save your pet's life? How much money would you be willing to spend to save your spouse's pet's life?

If your partner feels the pet is getting more of your attention than he is, does the pet go?

When your pet ultimately dies, will you replace it? If yes, with what? If yes, how soon would you replace your pet?

POLITICS

Do you vote in local, state and national elections? If yes, how regularly? If no, why not?

Would you describe yourself as conservative or liberal?

Do you belong to a political party? If yes, which one?

Do you consider yourself politically active? If yes, how active? How much time do you devote to politics each month? How much time would you like to devote?

Would you like to run for public office one day? If yes, what office?

Would you object to your spouse belonging to a different political party than you do? Will you mind if your spouse votes for an opposing candidate to yours?

POLITICS, cont.

What services should the government provide? Not provide?

PRIVACY & SECRETS

With whom will you share details of your personal married life (e.g., disagreements, secrets, successes) once you are married? Parents? Friends? Co-workers? Your children? What kinds of details are okay to share with these people? Which topics, if any, are not okay to share with others?

Is it acceptable to have a part of your life that you are intentionally not sharing with your partner? If yes, about what general topics (e.g., past relationships, phone calls with ex-spouse, what you do when you're with your friends)?

Does your job require discretion or secrecy? If yes, why?

Does your job put you or your family in danger? If yes, how?

RELIGION

What role did religion play in your family life when you were growing up? To which religious group did your family belong?

Do you believe in a Supreme Being? If yes, what name do you use to refer to the Supreme Being?

What role does religion play in your life now? To which religious group(s) do you belong? How often do you attend services? How much time do you donate to your religious group each month? Do you say grace at meals? Do you pray regularly? Is it important that your spouse join you in these activities?

Do you want your spouse to convert to your religion? If yes, when? How important is your spouse's conversion to you?

Do you want to be married in a religious service? If yes, who will officiate? Do you want to be married in a religious building?

RELIGION, cont.

What role do you see religion playing in your marriage? What expectations does your religion place on your marriage? How important are these expectations to you?

How would you feel if your spouse decided to join a religious organization other than the one to which you belong?

How would you feel if your spouse changed religious affiliation (e.g. from Christianity to Buddhism, from Methodist to Unitarian or from Reform to Orthodox)? Dropped all religious affiliation?

ROLES

Which of the following roles are you expecting to play in your marriage? Which are you expecting your spouse to play? If you don't plan to have either of you do these things, who will do them? Arbitrator for children? Auto mechanic? Bed maker? Bookkeeper? Breadwinner? Comedian? Companion? Cook? Dish washer? Errand runner? Friend? Grounds keeper? Hair stylist? Handyman? Host/Hostess? Housekeeper? Laundress? Lover? Maid? Nanny? Nurse? Parent? Secretary? Shopper? Snow shoveler? Status symbol? Taxi driver for children? Travel agent?

ROUTINES - WORK DAY MORNING

What time do you get out of bed? For what time is the alarm set?

What is your routine from the first time the alarm goes off until you are out the door? Note approximate times for each step.

Outline a typical day from the time you leave the house until you arrive back home. If you are home during the day, describe how your time is spent and approximate times for each activity. If you have once a week chores, when do you generally handle them?

ROUTINES - WORK DAY EVENING

What is your routine from the time you get home until bedtime?

What is your routine from the time you get home until bedtime on Friday night? How would you like to spend Friday night?

ROUTINES - SATURDAY (or first day off work)

What is your Saturday routine? Outline your typical Saturday giving approximate times for each activity. How would you like to spend Saturday? How would you like to spend Saturday night?

ROUTINES - SUNDAY (or second day off work)

What is your Sunday routine? Outline your typical Sunday giving approximate times for each activity. How would you like to spend Sunday?

ROUTINES - SLEEP

What side of the bed do you sleep on? What is your sleeping position (on back, left or right side, stomach)?

If your spouse wants to put an arm around you in the night, do you think this will be okay with you?

How long does it generally take you to fall asleep?

Do you have difficulty staying asleep? If yes, explain.

If you have difficulty sleeping, what steps have you taken to improve your sleep patterns?

Do you get up during the night to go to the bathroom? If yes, how many times and when?

Do you expect to sleep in the same bed as your spouse? If yes, what size bed do you plan to share? If no, will your beds be in the same room?

Do you expect that you and your spouse will go to bed at the same

ROUTINES - SLEEP, cont.

time every night. If yes, at what time? If no, when do you think each of you will go to bed?

Do you snore? Do you toss and turn? If your sleep habits keep your spouse from getting a good night sleep, which of the following would you consider?

Getting professional help for your sleep patterns?

Getting professional help for spouse's sleep problems?

Sleeping in separate beds in same room?

Sleeping in separate rooms?

SEX

What are some things you find attractive about your spouse? What could your partner do to be even more attractive to you?

Will you discuss your sexual relationship with your spouse - what pleases you, what you would like him to do or not do?

What are you willing to do? Not willing to do?

If your partner wants to tell you something about your sexual relationship, when, where and how is the best way to approach you?

Are you a virgin? What sexual experience have you had?

Do you have any illnesses or take medications which may affect sexual performance? If yes, explain

Do you have any sexual fantasies? If yes, do you hope to act them out? What role do you hope your partner will play in your fantasies? What if your partner doesn't want to act out your fantasies?

In your mind, are the following having sex? Touching breasts? Touching genitals? Oral sex? Anal sex? Phone sex? On-line sex? Intimate touching through clothing? Reading or viewing pornography? Sexual conduct with someone of same sex?

Will you/spouse be sexually exclusive to each other? What does this mean to you?

SEX, cont.

Is it okay if your spouse does any of the following with someone other than you? Have intercourse? Lingering kiss? French kiss? Touch breasts? Touch genitals? Oral sex? Anal sex? Phone sex? On-line sex? Intimate touching through clothing? Reading or viewing pornography? Massage (non sexual areas)?

What impact do you think it would have on your marriage if your partner did any of those previous things with someone other than you? Do you think it would end your marriage?

How frequently do you envision having sex after marriage?

Are you willing to try a "never say no to sex" policy in your marriage?
If yes, what guidelines would you expect? (e.g., times or places that would always be off limits, for example, public places)
If no, what will you do when you want sex but your partner's not in the mood? What if your partner wants sex but not you?

Who will initiate sex? How may sex be initiated? Touch? Ask?

Do you masturbate? If yes, will you masturbate when married?

Have you ever used a vibrator or other sexual aid? Would you be willing to try these if your partner wanted to try them?

Have you ever had an orgasm? If yes, do you come to climax easily?
If no, how do you feel when you don't climax? What can your partner do to help you climax?

Do you now have or have you ever had herpes? Genital warts? Gonorrhea, syphilis or other sexually transmitted disease? A test for AIDS or HIV? What was the test result? Have you ever been exposed to AIDS or HIV?

Would you like you and your partner to be tested for AIDS or HIV?

SKELETONS IN YOUR CLOSET

Is there anything anyone has on you that they could use as blackmail? If yes, are you willing to disclose it to your partner?

Are there any irritating or embarrassing stories your spouse will hear from family, friends, co-workers? If yes, explain.

Is there anything in your past you're ashamed of? If yes, explain.

Anything you wish were different about you? If yes, explain.

In your family, are there any incidents of child abuse? Child abuser? Abuse of drugs or alcohol? Serious illness? Legal problems? Jail time? Bankruptcy? Divorce?

Is there someone in your family you'd prefer your partner not meet? If yes, who is this? Why don't you want them to meet? How likely is it that your partner will meet him?

What things have you been avoiding telling your partner?

SMOKING

Do either you or your spouse either currently or did you previously: Smoke cigarettes? Cigar? Pipe? Marijuana? Chew tobacco?

SMOKING - SMOKERS

Will you stop smoking during spouse's pregnancy?

Will you smoke after you have children?

Would you be willing to smoke only outside?

Would you like to stop smoking? If yes, what are you willing to do to stop smoking?

What if your smoking partner stops smoking?

SMOKING - NON-SMOKERS

Are you bothered by smoking?

Will you ask your partner not to smoke in the house? Will you ask

SMOKING - NON-SMOKERS, cont.

guests not to smoke in your home?

What if your non-smoking partner starts smoking?

SUPPORT

What ways does your partner currently show support for your efforts that you especially appreciate? What things are you currently doing to demonstrate your support for your partner's efforts?

In what areas is your partner's support most important to you? What can your partner do to show his support?

TALENTS

What are your personal strengths?

What skills are you most proud of?

What skills would you like to develop further? How can your spouse support your efforts?

TELEPHONE

Do you like to talk on the phone? How much time do you spend on the phone each day at home?

Are there any people you talk to regularly? If yes, to whom? How often? For how long?

Do you plan to change your telephone habits once you're married? If yes, explain.

Do you have a cell phone? Does your partner? If yes, will you keep your cell phone once you marry? Will your partner keep his?

In addition to any cell phones you have, how many land phone lines will you have? Will you have a separate children's line?

Who will answer the phone? What greeting will they use? Will you have an answering machine?

Who will you call long distance on your home phone?

THESE ARE A FEW OF MY FAVORITE THINGS

Candy? Car? Color? Flower? Type of Jewelry? Meal? Snack? Treat? Memory? Musical Group? Night Out? Number? Song?

What are some of your other favorite things? Do you want your spouse to share these favorite things with you? If yes, how can your spouse share these with you?

Do you like to shop? If yes, for what? How often do you like to go shopping?

THINGS YOU CAN DO TO SHOW ME YOU'RE SORRY

Sometimes it's difficult to be the first to say you're sorry - or to accept your spouse's apology. You may find it helpful to identify things you can do for each other to help salve the wounds - like buying a pint of your favorite ice cream or picking up a paperback by a favorite author. What are some small things your spouse might do for you as an opening to an apology?

If you have difficulty finding the right words but don't want things to drag on as long as it might take to locate a pint of ice cream or an open bookstore, you may find it helpful to agree on a small gesture you can make to show your spouse you're ready to talk and clear the air. A simple but unusual action will work well - like wearing a safety pin on your collar or placing a dinner plate on the coffee table. The act itself is not important; the significance the two of you give it is.

THINGS WE LIKE TO DO TOGETHER

List dozens of things. It probably won't seem possible, but the day will probably come when you'll be bored silly and unable to think of anything fun to do. Having this list can bring back great memories and set off delightful escapades.

THE MARRIAGE PACT™ QUESTIONNAIRE

TRADING FACES
What planned deceits have you put on for your partner?
Note: A planned deceit is something you would not normally do that you do specifically because you think it makes you more attractive to your partner. See Trading Faces, Clue #4. Examples might be always wearing makeup, staying dressed up after work, keeping your home spotless, spending time with partner's family.
Are you planning to stop any of these when you marry? Which ones?

UNEMPLOYMENT
Have you ever been unemployed? If yes, what were the circumstances? How did you feel? Did you qualify to collect unemployment? Did you collect unemployment? If no, why not?
Are you likely to be unemployed in the future? Explain. How would the bills get paid if you/spouse were unemployed?
If you were laid off, would you file for unemployment? Explain.

UPDATING YOUR MARRIAGE PACT™
How often will you review your entire Marriage Pact™?
If your partner feels part of your Marriage Pact™ is not working, when, where and how is the best way to approach you on this subject? How quickly will you commit to review this portion of your Marriage Pact™? Remember - no pressure or guilt trips allowed!

VACATIONS
How much paid vacation time do you get? How would you like to spend your vacation time? Where would you like to spend your vacation? How important is going away on vacation to you?
Will you vacation separately, as a couple, with family or friends?
Will you take big vacations or little weekend getaways?
How often will you take little weekend getaways? What is your idea

246

VACATIONS, cont.

of a great weekend getaway?

How often will you take big budget vacations? What is your idea of a well-spent big budget vacation?

How would you like to travel on vacation? Car? Train? Bus? House boat? Cruise ship? Other boat? Plane? Other?

If you had to choose between buying a house (or other large purchase) or taking nice vacations, which would you choose?

VEHICLES

Do you have a driver's license? Do you drive?

What kind of vehicle(s) are you licensed to drive?

Have you ever had an accident? If yes, explain.

How many of the following do you currently own or want to own? Cars, Trucks, Vans, RV, Boats, Motorcycles, Planes, ATV.

How often should you be able to get a different vehicle?

How often should your spouse be able to get a different vehicle?

Do you buy or lease your vehicles? Why?

When you buy a vehicle, do you pay cash or buy on credit?

Do you buy/lease new or used vehicles?

How much do you spend for a vehicle?

How important are your vehicles to you? How important are your vehicles to your job?

What type of vehicle do you expect to drive five years from now? Ten years? Twenty years?

WEDDING

What type of wedding do you want? Where would you like your wedding to be held? How many guests would you like to attend? What would you/spouse wear at your wedding? How many bridesmaids and groomsmen would you have?

WEDDING, cont.

What kind of wedding do your parents want for you? How important are their wishes to you?

Who will pay for your wedding? What can the person paying for the wedding afford to spend on the wedding?

If the person paying for the wedding wants a different wedding than you do, would you consider paying for the wedding yourself so you can have what you want?

Are you willing to go into debt for your wedding? If yes, how much debt are you willing to incur? How will you pay off this debt and how long will it take?

If someone offered you cash to elope rather than have a formal wedding, would you take it? How much cash would they have to offer, for you to be willing to forego a formal wedding?

Whom do you want to attend your wedding?

Whom do you want in your wedding party? Whose feelings will be hurt if they are not included in your wedding party?

Will you wear a wedding ring? Will your spouse wear a wedding ring? If you don't plan to wear a ring and your spouse wants you to wear a wedding ring, will you wear one? If no, why not?

Do you want to take a honeymoon? If yes, where would you like to go? How long would you like to be gone? How much can you afford to spend on a honeymoon?

Are you ready to get married now? If not, when will you be ready?

WELFARE

Have you ever been on welfare? If yes, when? What were the circumstances? How did you feel about being on welfare?

What are your thoughts on use/abuse of the welfare system?

What are your thoughts on use/abuse of food stamps?

PART VI

ADDITIONAL RESOURCES
FOR
MASTERING MARRIAGE

INCLUDING SOME
GREAT FREE STUFF

FREE BONUS GIFTS FOR OUR READERS

As a "Thank You" for reading this book, and to additionally assist you in implementing the clues, we'd like to give you three special reports packed with more strategies and ideas for growing happier and more in love each year - FREE!

- *Is It Ever Okay to Say No to Sex?* This report answers one of the biggest questions we get. It guides you through a conversation with your partner as you discover the answers you need to keep your sex life and marriage strong.
- *Why You May Not Want to Be the Ideal Spouse.* Some couples find that the harder they try, the worse things get in their relationship. This special report reveals a common mistake couples make and how to avoid it.
- *Balancing Work and Family, Strategies that Work.* This report gives practical advice to give your relationship its proper priority while still reaching your career goals.

Open your gifts at: **www.MasteringMarriage.com/ReaderGifts**
or submit the following form (photocopy okay):

FREE Gift Request Form

Yes, Charlie & Mike - please send me my three free bonus reports plus a free subscription to your **Marriage Masters**™ email newsletter where I can learn tips other couples use to grow their love and share ideas that are working for us. *I know you'll always respect my email privacy and I can unsubscribe anytime.*

Name_____

Address_____

City_____ State_____ Zip_____

Email_____

Wedding Date (month)_____(day)_____(year)_____

Fax completed form to 614-340-0806   **or**
Mail to: Mastering Marriage, PO Box 1766, Westerville, OH 43086

ANOTHER FREEBIE!

Join MARRIAGE MASTERS™ at **www.MarriageMasters.com**
The free Web site for happy couples by happy couples™
(Note-this is different than the site for Mastering Marriage product sales.)

Tap into tips and techniques to keep you happy and in love for a lifetime. Whether you are engaged, newlyweds, married with children, re-married or empty nesters, there is something for everybody.

Share ideas and successes with other happy couples:
- Things you wish you'd known before you married.
- Time-saving tips to give you more time for family.
- How you make time for just the two of you.
- Daily rituals you use to keep love alive.
- Holiday traditions to successfully blend your families.
- Activities you'd like to share with couples in your area.
- Great date ideas.
- Money-saving tips so you have more money to save or spend.
- Romantic getaways that won't break the bank.
- Child rearing tips to maintain control and sanity.
- Cooking tips and favorite, time-saving recipes.
- Getting reacquainted after the children leave.
- Anniversary gifts from corporate sponsors.

Get your **free** subscription to Marriage Masters email newsletter with relationship bolstering tips, techniques and just plain good information.

Support happy marriages. Let's make it fashionable to be "happily married and proud of it™." Invite friends and family to join, too.

ADDITIONAL PRODUCTS

The Marriage Pact™ Questionnaire Workbook (soft cover)
The 8½" x 11" format lies flat for easy writing and lists each question with ample space for answers, notes and comments. Save time and simplify the process by eliminating the need to copy the numerous questions into a notebook. Keep your thoughts organized. $22.95

The Marriage Pact™ Questionnaire eBook Workbook (eBook)
Avoid handwriting all together! Fill in the answers on your computer. Please visit **www.MasteringMarriage.com/Products** for details.

Our Marriage Pact™ (hard cover)
Formalize your Marriage Pact™ in style. This beautiful, royal blue hardbound volume is embossed with gold lettering proclaiming "Our Marriage Pact™". As practical as it is handsome, the 8½" x 11" book lies flat for easy writing. It lists all the questions with space to enter your agreements. Give your pact a durable place of honor. $25.95

Mastering Marriage (hard cover)
The perfect gift for bridal showers, weddings and anniversaries. The impact of this book will last years longer than a toaster. The most thoughtful gift you can give a couple you care about. $19.95

Mastering Marriage, Combined Edition (soft cover)
Combines the complete text of *Mastering Marriage* with the expanded questionnaire format of *The Marriage Pact™ Questionnaire Workbook* in a stay flat book. **Save $7.00** over individual books. $35.90

Books are available at **www.MasteringMarriage.com/Products,** by calling toll free **888-IPickYou (888-474-2596)**, or at your favorite bookstore. Prices are subject to change without notice.

For Special Deals on Combination Packages of Books and Work-books and for Audio, Video & Teleseminar Products please visit **www.MasteringMarriage.com/Products**

Please **call** Mastering LifeSkills Inc. at 614-334-6627 to discuss your interests and requirements for the following products and services:

Fundraising & Group Sales
Raise money for your organization by helping couples strengthen their relationships. Special discounts are available to religious organizations, schools, marriage professionals, Marriage Masters™ groups, educational programs and for business promotions.

Presentations, Workshops, Keynotes, Couples Coaching
Designed to meet the needs of individual clients.

WE'D LOVE TO HEAR FROM YOU!

CONTRIBUTE YOUR FEEDBACK ON *Mastering Marriage*
Please help us make future editions as helpful as possible by sharing:
- What you liked most about the book.
- Topics you discussed as you prepared your Marriage Pact™ that were not covered in the book.
- Which clues you feel will have the most positive effect on your relationship.
- Your own special "clues" that help keep the love alive in your relationship.
- An example of how the book has helped you.
- Your suggestions to improve future editions.
- Your review of the book.

Please visit **www.MasteringMarriage.com**, click "Reader Input" and share your thoughts and opinions. A **prize** will be awarded for the best suggestion received each month.

OUR SIGNATURE PROGRAMS

Are you serious about giving your relationship top priority? Join us for a relaxing, get-away weekend. Spend three days with Mike and Charlie. See the clues lived daily. Practice them first hand. Ask questions and get answers. Spend time with other happy couples who want to make their relationship the best it can be.

Dream Building Weekend for Engaged Couples
You will never have a second chance to start your marriage off right. During three stimulating days, you will lay the foundation on which to build your future together. Define the unique course that is right for the two of you. Focus on your marriage, not your wedding. Learn how to turn your marriage into a lifelong love affair.

From Newly Wed to Happily Wed
Smooth the transition from "I do" to "We do." In just three days you can align your expectations into the reality of your marriage. Ensure that both of you find what you are looking for in your relationship. Increase intimacy, understanding, communication, passion and personal satisfaction. Learn simple tools to stay in tune with each other and grow your love and happiness daily.

Relationship Rejuvenating Weekend for Married Couples
With so many things vying for your attention, it's easy for the most important relationship in your life to get shortchanged. Don't let this happen to you. Love doesn't disappear overnight, but it can fade a little each day. Keep your love vibrant. Take the time you need together. Your marriage not only deserves your priority, it requires nurturing to stay fresh, passionate and fulfilling. Join us for a three day weekend of reconnecting and revitalization. Focus on each other and your future. Create the marriage you want right in the middle of the marriage you have. Leave with simple techniques you will apply daily to keep your love growing stronger every day.

Visit **www.MasteringMarriage.com/Weekend** for details.